A COOL, fRESH, PHaT

SLANGuage

AND SHaGaDELiC Guide

to All Kinds of SLANG

MIKE ELLIS

HYPERION

NEW YORK

Book design by Ruth Lee

Library of Congress Cataloging-in-Publication Data

Ellis, Mike, 1961–
    Slanguage : a cool, fresh, phat, and shagadelic guide to all kinds of
slang / Mike Ellis.
        p. cm.
    ISBN: 0-7868-8520-3
    1. English Language—Slang—Glossaries, vocabularies, etc.
I. Title.

PE3721 .E45 2000
427'.09—dc21
                                                            00-025696

2   4   6   8   10   9   7   5   3   1

taBLE of ConTENts

EVERY AMERICAN CITY'S SLANGUAGE   135

FOREIGN SLANGUAGES   139

GENERATIONAL SLANGUAGE   187

TEENAGE SLANGUAGE   197

RECREATIONAL SLANGUAGE   237

OCCUPATIONAL SLANGUAGES   249

SLANGUAGE CROSSWORD PUZZLES   259

iNTRoDucTion

Slanguage was born in 1974 on a junior high school bus. A dude we'll call Dave Now helped create slanguage by tossing an egg salad (some say tuna salad) hoagie out the bus window in the direction of a passing Volkswagen. Neither Johnny U nor Roman Gabriel could've thrown a more perfect spiral. The hoagie (if you're not from the Philadelphia area, hoagies are sub sandwiches) exploded on the Volkswagen's windshield. We cheered as Cuda, our aptly named bus driver, continued driving, unaware of what caused all the commotion.

Cuda found out about the hoagie at the next bus stop, when the irate driver boarded our bus demanding to know what was all over his car. This made Cuda sigh, as she was clueless as to the flying hoagie. Fortunately, especially for Dave Now, the man left without incident.

Years later, while employed at a financial exchange in Chicago that often hosted Japanese tourists, I overheard a translater say "Cuda Sigh." I learned that "Cuda Sigh" in Japanese means please.

This hoagie-tossing experience taught me that foreign languages can be taught using English. With slanguage, you too can easily learn a language—from another town, country, culture, job, generation or recreation. Since all languages can be taught as English, maybe slanguage is the beginning of the end of all language barriers.

At about the same bat time on a different bat channel in a nearby junior high school, a young gentleman named Stix Neltone was about to make slanguage history in a way that he would have preferred to have done differently. Unfortunately, at that time, there was no *Slanguage* book available to help Stix.

Stix, a world-class drummer and Senior PGA Tour hopeful, had just moved to the Philadelphia area from Michigan. Unbeknownst to Stix, he possessed a strong Midwestern accent. One day in math class, Stix, on a mission to impress the beautiful and well-tanned Joanna Rigatoni, enthusiastically responded to his math teacher's question, "What is the area of a circle?" "Pie AIR squared," exclaimed Stix, eyeing up his beloved Miss Rigatoni. Stix's pride and happiness were quickly squelched and turned to unhappiness and embarrassment when the entire eighth-grade math class started barking at him, "AIR AIR AIR!!!"

Stix didn't raise his hand for a long time after that. Had Stix owned and utilized a *Slanguage* book back in 1974, he would have known that a Philadelphia-area student might say "pie OR squared" for the area of a circle. If Stix had possessed a *Slanguage* book, it might have changed history for the better. *Slanguage* would have made Stix an instant insider—talking like the locals—unafraid to speak his mind. Like it should be.

As a kid growing up in a large, Italian family, I was exposed to languages at an early age. I easily remember talking to my grandfather when I was at most five or six. Since he didn't speak English (except for "Petty Co," for Perry Como), I learned a few phrases using my own method. "Bonus Sarah" to me meant good evening to my grandfather. He always asked me "COMB messed ah?" and I knew "Benny" was the response. He asked me "How are you?" and I responded, "Fine." Little did I know that my own method for teaching myself languages would someday be published by Hyperion.

I liked learning languages throughout school, but the way they taught us was boring and repetitive. It wasn't until I went to Penn State and took some linguistics and phonetics courses that I discovered what I was doing inside my head. Always a good listener, I was breaking down phrases and words into their most basic syllables, or phonemes. Listening to languages, all I heard were these phonemes such as key, comb, bell, toe and on and on forever.

After college, I spent a year working in Europe, mostly in southern France. Strangely, I could speak the language very quickly, but had trouble understanding the language. Most Americans find it easier to understand the language, then later learn how to speak it. I often taught other English-speaking people how to speak French while working with them, and they marveled at my method. It wasn't until a few years later that I realized that I had a new method for teaching people.

My experience at the Chicago financial exchange was the moment that I realized that I did have an idea that might be valuable to many people.

Upon returning from Chicago, I set out to teach people languages via a small series of books I self-published. I initially called my method linguistics engineering. It converted foreign languages into English so that enyone could learn any language. It was met with a little success—some sales, distribution and media coverage.

The name was soon changed to FUNICS because too many people thought that linguistics engineering was too serious a name and it implied a process that wasn't what I was trying to do. FUNICS soon got a huge jump start when I applied my teaching methods to something never before published, but everybody understood—how to speak Philadelphian.

Spring of 1993 was fun. *Philly Funics, Yuze Can Speak Philadelphian* was launched with much fanfare—dozens of plugs in the local media as well as national and international stories in *USA Today* and on popular television shows such as *American Journal*. Thirty-thousand copies sold merely whetted my appetite—what did people say in other cities and countries around the world?

It wasn't until spring 1996 that I launched my website SLANGUAGE, http://www.slanguage.com. Finally, a vehicle for collecting and enjoying slang, colloquialisms and lingo from people around the world. Give away a free *Philly Funics* book and people will send you their best stuff. A couple million visitors later, and I have one of the best collections of topical, updated slang in the world.

November 1997 was also huge. I got a plug in the Sunday *New York Times* by a gentleman originally from Philadelphia named Joe Sharkey. I heard from many people, including several major New York City publishers. They all asked, "Do you have an agent?" Joe Sharkey referred me to his superstar agent David Vigliano. I think it's great that David's client list includes Blondie, Randall Cunningham, Rick Pitino, Grace Slick, then me. I guess I have nowhere to go but up. Many thanks to David and his staff. Also a big thanks to Alex Smithline.

The best thing about slanguage is that this book is only the tip of the iceberg. More and more people keep visiting slanguage dot com. My collection of slanguage will grow forever. As we continue to expand slanguage beyond regional slanguage to include recreational, occupational and generational slanguage, it's easy to see how slanguage could become one of the largest collections of slang ever.

You'll notice a lot of slanguage for Philadelphia and the surrounding areas. Since I'm from there, it was easy to collect the local slanguage. I think it's also important to show others how strong the accent really is in this area. There are many who don't think Philadelphians have an accent at all. Just ask them what H_2O stands for. When they say "wooder," you'll see what I mean. I also like "Hail nail braille'n kale" for How now brown cow. You gotta admit it's beauty-full! Come to Fluffya (local speak for Philadelphia) and see the Iggles, eat some scrapple and go to the Dad Vail. Know the difference between ice wooder and wooder ice. Find King a Presha, Manuyunk and The Main Loin on a map. Yo, Adrian!

You'll see a lot of call outs (sidebars if you're a publisher) throughout my book that emphasize a phrase or two from each city. Use them to help yourself talk like a local in that city. Instant gratification slanguistically. Ain't nothin' better for turning you from hick to hip.

The future looks bright for slanguage. The current globalization trend makes it more and more important to be able to communicate with people, no matter where they're from.

Someday in the not-too-distant future, we'll be traveling via the space shuttle to places all over the globe. It will be imperative that one can communicate with dozens of people in different countries who don't speak American. *Slanguage* will enable us to speak many many languages without effort. Since we now know that all languages are really English anyway, why not start learning to speak these languages now?

AMERiCAN CiTies

Albany, New York

MISCELLANEOUS SLANGUAGE

Awbny how the locals pronounce the name of their town

Rinsler how the locals pronounce the name of the town across the river (Rensselaer)

Soon yah S.U.N.Y.A. (the State University of New York at Albany)

Calla KNEE Colonie, a suburb

Ro ZELL ville Roessleville, yet another suburb

Vuh LAY shuh Valatie, a nearby town

Scatta Coke Sgachticoke, a nearby town

Northway Interstate 87 from Albany to the Canadian border

True way Interstate 87 south to New York City and Interstate 90 west to Buffalo

The Track August racing meet at Saratoga Race Track

The City New York City

Spack Saratoga Performing Arts Center

Egg big "arts center" in the middle of Albany

Pepsi arena in downtown Albany . . . not soda

River Rots our hockey team

Anchorage, Alaska

Nickname Los Anchorage is our Californicated nickname.

Most popular phrase "Go home, you forty-niner" (Go home, tourist)

Well-known spot Koots, nickname for a local bar, Chilkoot Charlies

Popular sport/leisure combat fishing. We enjoy the elbow-to-elbow fishing conditions at popular fishing spots.

MISCELLANEOUS SLANGUAGE

Honeybucket outdoor plumbing

Tundra No. 9 those moose nuggets

Sourdough someone who is sour on Alaska and doesn't have the money to leave the state

Cheechako someone who has been in Alaska less than one year

Winter roads frozen rivers approved by the state as part of the highway system

Juneau where we keep our politicians isolated from the rest of the people

The Chain the Aleutian Islands

Mukluks snow boots

RATNET defunct television network outside Alaska's big cities

Snowmachine snowmobile

Spenard divorce (Spenard is a part of Anchorage) a divorce by shotgun

Alaska tax higher markup on products because of shipping to Alaska

Mucktuck drunk native of Alaska

Ann Arbor, Michigan

Nickname A Squared

Well-known spot In the summer everyone vacations UP NORTH—north of Clare, MI

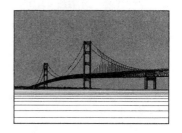

Popular sport/leisure attending Michigan Wolverine football games

MISCELLANEOUS SLANGUAGE

Michiganders people who live here

Big Mac Mackinac Bridge

The U name for the University of Michigan

Moo U derisive nickname for Michigan State University, the aggie school to the north

The Big House nickname for Michigan Stadium, the largest on-campus football stadium in the United States

Yostmen nickname for Michigan hockey fans

The Morgue nickname for Crisler Arena, because of its poor lighting and dead crowds for basketball

The Great White North nickname for the North Campus section of U of M

Mawklee nickname given by native Michiganders to Markley Hall, home to many, many students from the East Coast

The UGLI the undergraduate library, which has UGLI stamped on its bookends

Whackcess the annoying name for Wolverine Access, the website of the Office of the Registrar

The Mental Ward nickname for Couzens Hall, which is rumored to have been the university hospital's sanatarium at the turn of the twentieth century

MoJo nickname for Mosher-Jordan Hall

The Diag the heart of campus, with pathways which run outward from it diagonally

Hale Boppers those who dance in honor of Alan Hale Jr. during the *Gilligan's Island* theme song

Atlanta, Georgia

Nicknames Phatlanta, Hotlanta, It-lanna

Most popular phrase "Love them Goo Goo Clusters." They're a regional candy made from chocolate and peanuts.

BETTY BUCKHEAD

Famous local food Get a lube job. It's an actual meal at the famous Varsity restaurant. A few chili cheese dogs are guaranteed to clean out your digestive tract.

Well-known spot The Big Chicken is a popular landmark in nearby Marietta.

Popular sport/leisure You can't go to Atlanta without seeing a Braves game at the Ted and doing the chop. So what if it's not so politically correct?

MISCELLANEOUS SLANGUAGE

Mash the button Press the button.

Goody patters Goody powders, like aspirin

Buggies shopping carts

Ass burn take it for a headache

The Varsity a popular restaurant

Co Cola and a Moon Pie an Atlanta meal

Get a lube job Go to the Varsity and eat a few chili cheese dogs.

Gem clips paper clips

Bagga ass a bag of ice

Atlanter our town

Shoot the hooch ride a raft down the Chatahoochee River

The Perimeter freeway that circles the city, also known as 1285

Hartsfield Intergalactic Atlanta's airport

Betty Buckhead woman in the Buckhead community who loves to shop

Connector place where two freeways blend into one as I-85 and I-75 do

Topside northern part of the Perimeter, where most of the newer developments and traffic are. Along the same vein: "Heartlanta" for inside, "Outlanta" for outside the Perimeter.

Butt Head another name for the pseudo-hip Buckhead

Stop and Rob a convenience store

The PIB acronym for Peachtree Industrial Boulevard

Bev's Boys Atlanta Police Department, led by Chief Beverly Harvard

The Ted Turner Field, home of the Atlanta Braves

The Cobb Web intersection of I-75 and I-285 in Cobb County

Pin something you write with

The Grady Curve often-bottlenecked area of the downtown connector in front of Grady Hospital

Ear bobs Earrings

A quota 25-cent piece!

The High the High Museum of Art

Fur red what my niece in Atlanta calls her husband, Fred

Little Five downtown district with shopping and food

The Autobahn Interstate 85

The Buck Buckhead district (bars and rich people)

Underground remains of the old town not burnt by Sherman, preserved intact underground

Auburn, Alabama

Most popular phrase "War damn Eagle," Auburn battle cry, taunt, and greeting to fellow Auburn men and women

Well-known spot The Club is the nickname for popular waterin' hole The War Eagle Supper Club.

Popular sport/leisure The Tiger Walk is the gameday ritual of thousands of fans, who line the streets from the athletic dorm to the stadium to wish the football team well on their way to the game.

MISCELLANEOUS SLANGUAGE

Buck Fama popular phrase used to show the special relationship Auburn people have for the "other" university in the state (BAMA)

Keebler affectionate nickname for small-of-stature football coach Terry Bowden

Bubba another name for a Bama student

Corona, Cartman, and Conflict term for Wednesday night ritual of curling a few cold ones and watching *South Park*, followed by the ever popular Jerry Springer "too hot for TV" video

Austin, Texas

Most popular phrase "Dellionaires" is the nickname for the first thousand employees working for Dell computer, who were made exceedingly wealthy by the stock option plan.

Well-known spot In 1966, Austin became famous for "the shooting"— the infamous shooting off the UT tower by a former student, who killed 19 people.

MISCELLANEOUS SLANGUAGE

The Drag the part of Guadalupe Street that borders the University of Texas

The big parking lot Interstate 35

Sixth the street between 5th Street and 7th Street, lined with bars

You Tee University of Texas

Good-bye and good luck the last thing every student hears when registering by phone

Drag Worm homeless person living on Guadalupe Street

Ags or Aggies nickname for the students of Texas A&M University

T-sips nickname for the students of the University of Texas at Austin

Baltimore, Maryland

Nickname Ball Mer

Most popular phrase "Hi, hon" is the most popular greeting here.

Famous local food crabs, crabs and mo' crabs

Well-known spot Every summer, thousands of folks here go "downey OWE shin" (to the beach).

Popular sport/leisure watching the O's at our beauty-full, new Memorial stadium

MISCELLANEOUS SLANGUAGE

Ball Mer Orals our baseball team

Droodle Pork Druid Hill Park

Simonize Hospital Sinai Hospital

Balmoreese what we speak

The Oreos not a cookie, but our baseball team

Low Hon a greeting

Chess Peek a big bay

Natie Bow our preferred beer

Tapsico River Patapsco River

Jayf X Highway 83, the JFX, or Jones Falls Expressway

Balmorons how the natives refer to themselves

Chikkin Nekkers recreational crabber

Curl Park Carroll Park

Hawkins Johns Hopkins Hospital

Demos another word for our baseball team, as in, "How bow demos!"

Granite granted ("take it for granite")

Wooder what the Chess Peek is made of

Bar Harbor, Maine

Nickname Bah Hobba is the correct way to pronounce the name of our town.

Most popular phrase "You Mainiac. Go back to Disgusta."

Famous local food Boy Gawd, we love to eat lobstas.

Well-known spot Disgusta is our state capital.

MISCELLANEOUS SLANGUAGE

Ban gowah Bangor

Brewa neighboring city of Brewer

Raw bit a man's name

Puckerbrush any prickly plants like raspberries; also a reference to the countryside ("He lives in the puckerbrush")

Beverly Hills, California

MISCELLANEOUS SLANGUAGE

Little Santa Monica Santa Monica Boulevard

FOB (fresh off the boat) recent Russian or Iranian immigrant

BHHS our famous high school

The Hills that's our town

Hillbillies a not-so-flattering nickname for us

The Ghetto any part of town south of Wilshire Boulevard

Oy vey! "Oh, no" in Yiddish

Hafeyshoht "Shut up" in Farsi

Binghamton, New York

Nicknames Bingo Town, The Ham.

We are located in the Suck a Banana Valley (Susquehanna Valley).

Most popular phrase "Yo zipperhead. Go back to work." A zipperhead is an IBM employee.

Famous local food Speedies are skew-
ered cubes of meat grilled on an
open flame, sort of like a kabob.

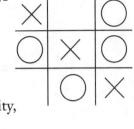

Well-known spot the Triple Cities
(refers to the "metropolitan"
area of Binghamton, Johnson City,
and Endicott)

Popular sport/leisure "Shapping" is our way of saying shopping.

MISCELLANEOUS SLANGUAGE

The Southern Tier refers to the Binghamton area's location in
southern Central New York State

EN dee cat Endicott

SUE knee refers to the State University of New York Binghamton campus

BO chee someone who attends BOCES, a vocational training
program

Pee AY Pennsylvania

Sarah cuse nearby city of Syracuse

Foyer fire

El MOY ra nearby city of Elmira

Birmingham, Alabama

Nicknames Magic City, Football Capital
of the South, The Ham

Most popular phrases "War Eagle" is the battle cry of Auburn fans. "Roll Tide" is the battle cry of Alabama fans.

Well-known spot The Five Points is a Southside area upon which all directions are based.

Popular sport/leisure Everyone who is anyone attends the Iron Bowl. It's the annual football game between Auburn and Alabama.

A city in the South known for its steel? Answer: The Ham

MISCELLANEOUS SLANGUAGE

Corridor X unfinished interstate system between Birmingham and Memphis

Goat Hill reference to the state capital of Montgomery

Malfunction Junction downtown interchange of I-65 and I-20/59

Over the Mountain wealthy suburbs south of Red Mountain

Vulcan large iron statue of the god of fire, atop Red Mountain

Moon over Homewood suburb of Homewood's view of Vulcan's bare backside

Boise, Idaho

Nicknames Boyzee 2 Men, Taterland

EYE dee hoe state we live in

Most popular phrase "I don't know"—what everyone from east of the Rockies thinks we're saying when we tell them where we're from. Calling someone a Mr. Potato

Head may not make you many
friends here.

Famous local food taters and
more Tater Tots

Well-known spot The Puzzle Palace is
the Idaho State capitol building.

Popular sport/leisure People rafting
the Boise River are commonly
called floaters.

**Mister
Potato Head
We Luv You**

Fort Simplot big mansion on the hill
owned by "Potato King" J.R. Simplot

The Flying Y intersection of I-84 and I-184.

Ideehoe the state we live in

Highlanders rich people

Microned anything or anyone that has been bought out by
MICRON Technologies

The Bench area of town above downtown

Boston, Massachusetts

Nickname Beantown is a popular name for
Boston in the state of Taxachussets.

Most popular phrase Begin all phrases with
"Boy Gawd. . . ." If someone is
going to the "potty," they are probably
going to a social event.

**TEA
POTTY**

Famous local food A spookie is a Boston sub
sandwich (from Italian spucadella).

Well-known spot The QUINN zee MACK it is one place where we shop outdoors.

Popular sport/leisure We love watching the Celts play at the God'n.

Best way to get punched in the face by a local Make jokes about the Red Sox's World Series record.

MISCELLANEOUS SLANGUAGE

1986 the year part of us died watching the World Series
Famine what farmers have been doing
Camel chewy stuff in some chocolate bars
Gaulic bread garlic bread
Collar woman's name (Carla)
Moniker another woman's name (Monica)
Uncle Bobbin Aunt Bob Uncle Bob and Aunt Barb

You have to pay attention when getting directions in Boston. The destinations aren't always pronounced as you might think.

Muhfuh Medford
Wuh Stuh Worcester
Pea Biddy Peabody
The Yad Harvard Yard
The Coop pronounced like "chicken coop," the Harvard Cooperative Society
Have Id Harvard
Pack Street Park Street
Mem Drive Memorial Drive

Dire rear an intestinal problem

Wicked tied very tired

God'n where the Celts play hoops

Dot Ave Dorchester Avenue

Packy where you buy liquor or a six-pack

Rozzie Roslindale (nice neighborhood)

So don't I So do I (our negative positive)

The T Boston subway

Triple Eagle one who attended B.C. High School, Boston
        College and B.C. law school

Boy Gawd By God

Draw drawer

Drawer to draw (a picture)

Roar bah raw bar

Awed opposite of even

Lodge budded pup con large buttered popcorn

Shock large, dangerous fish

Paw'p Tat quick breakfast food

Knee the rain Noah sleet what a Boston mailman might say

Boa not very exciting person

Noah nor, not the captain of the ark

Bonnie a purple dinosaur you probably detest

Oughta choke hats artichoke hearts

Spa Ma and Pa convenience store

Holly excellent motorcycle

Dorly Patton Dolly Parton

Lavish a sandwhich that is rolled in what looks to be similar
        to a square soft tortilla shell

Pru the second tallest building in New England

Broons the winners of too many to mention Stanley Cups

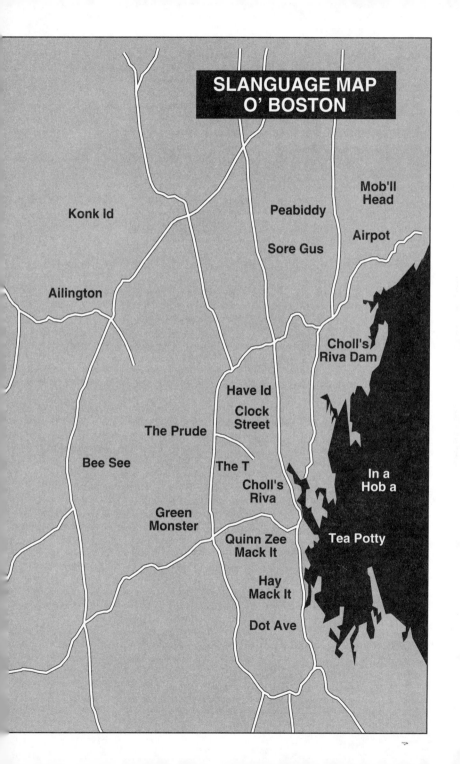

Wicked s'mat very intelligent

Easty Rat from East Boston

Da Patsies, P Men, Pats the New England Patriots

Nubbie Burger hamburger with egg and bacon

Bonnie derogatory term for a Harvard student in Boston

Mashin someone from Mars

Pack Street where the T's Red Line and Green Line intersect (Park Street)

Fennil Hall, Fenn Yil Hall local pronunciation of "Faneuil Hall," the name of a Revolutionary-era building (and tourist site), currently housing a number of boutiques

KWIN zee MACK it (Quincy Market) a Revolutionary-era closed market, currently the food court behind Faneuil Hall and serving the Faneuil Hall Marketplace (a couple of enclosed boutique malls behind Faneuil Hall)

HEY mack it the Haymarket, a weekend open-air green-market behind Quincy Market and Faneuil Hall Marketplace

Buffalo, New York

Nicknames Barfalo (repeating this at local bars may cause yourself serious harm)

Most popular phrase "Buffalo, a drinking town with a football problem" (again, this could get you in trouble)

Famous local food Buffalo Wings were born here at the Anchor Bar in 1964.

Well-known spot Schwabel's, where our local sandwich "Beef on Wek" originated

Popular sport/leisure waiting for the Bills to win the big one. We also take huge snowfalls in stride. Less than three feet and you're a wimp if you can't handle it.

MISCELLANEOUS SLANGUAGE

Canadian Ballet Buffalo strip joint

Mary on the half shell statue of Mary in half-buried clawfoot bathtub standing on end

Two-flat type of Buffalo housing

Wide right source of agony for anyone from Buffalo who remembers Superbowl XXV

Cheek a ta warsaw nickname for Cheektowaga, suburb of Buffalo whose inhabitants are mostly of Polish decent

Lego Land architectural description of the University of Buffalo, North Campus

'77 the year it REALLY snowed

Scajacuda (Ska JACK a dah) local highway

Also recall a failed hometown song that began "Boost Buffalo—it's good for you. . . ." but everyone sang "Booze Buffalo—it's good for you. . . ."

The NAP North Americare Park, the baseball park where the Buffalo Bisons play (formerly known as Pilot Field, until Pilot Air Freight defaulted on the contract for naming rights)

Bahama Police Buffalo Municipal Housing Authority (BMHA) police officers

Am I Gone funeral home common pronounciation for Amigone Funeral Homes, located throughout the city

The Youngman Route 290

The Kensington Route 33

Sponge candy a popular chocolate candy that does not contain any sponge

The Dominator Dominic Hasek

The Peace Bridge one of two bridges into Ft. Erie, Canada

Rich the stadium where the Bills play

Canton, Ohio

Tusc short for Tuscarawas, the main street that runs East and West through Canton

The Strip strip mall with a Wal-Mart, movie theater that has stadium seats, and Borders Books. Popular destination.

The Monument monument to President William McKinley

The Palace downtown theater that no one goes to

Tinseltown theater on the Strip that everyone goes to

Mother Goose Land abandoned children's amusement park that used to be close to the Monument. Still referred to by those who grew up here in the seventies and early eighties.

Pilot Knob gravel road in Middlebranch, outside North Canton, where people go to set off fireworks, make out, etc.

The Rep the *Repository*—crummy local paper that everyone reads, although no one ever admits to it

Charlotte, North Carolina

Nicknames The Queen City, SHAH Lot, Shawlet, Challot, SHALL it

Most popular phrase "Mash nine" will get you to the ninth floor of a building via the elevator.

Famous local food Livermush, a local food with a sausage texture made from pork liver, pork brains, pork spleen, and cornmeal

Well-known spot the South End, a trendy neighborhood of restaurants and shops

Popular sport/leisure making noise at the Hive, watching the Hornets. The Hive's Alive!

MISCELLANEOUS SLANGUAGE

Charlotteans natives of Charlotte

The Hive Charlotte Coliseum

The Square the official center of the city, the intersection of Trade and Tryon streets, uptown

You in sea sea University of North Carolina at Charlotte

Lyt bred white bread

Sun Drop local soft drink

Cheer whine Cheerwine, another local soft drink

Hose pop water hose (garden hose)

Rock Hillians (pronounced Rock Hilleans) people who live in Rock Hill, a South Carolina suburb of Charlotte

UCLA (University of Charlotte—'Lizabeth Avenue) for CPCC (Central Piedmont Community College), located on Elizabeth Avenue

Chicago, Illinois

Nicknames City of Broad Shoulders, Shy Town, Chicagoland, Windy City

Most popular phrase "I love Chicago." Chicagoans love their city with good reason. It's big, clean and there are lots of exciting things to do there. Chicagoans also have a difficult

time admitting to the existence of their strong accents. Johnny Carson has no accent. Chicagoans do!

Famous local food I-B's are local, delicious Italian beef sandwiches.

Well-known spot Broadcasting from high atop Da Cock, the John Hancock building.

Popular sport/leisure Da Cubs, Da Bears, Da Hocks, Da Sox, Da Bullz. Chicagoans love any and all sports with a passion.

Easy way to get your butt kicked Go to the Southside and praise the Cubs. If you're ignorant of the local teams, the Cubs are the Northside team of choice.

MISCELLANEOUS SLANGUAGE

Gangway narrow sidewalk between houses

Da Cock top of the Hancock Building

The Bubbly Creek Southside summer words for the Chicago River

Fronchroom Southside living room

The Wailing Wall walls outside the bleachers at Wrigley Field

The hock is out It's very windy.

CHICAGOANS DON'T HAVE ACCENTS: A STORY

I recently visited my friends in Chicago. They deny their accent exists. The slanguage below vividly demonstrates how strong their accent really is. The translations are below.

My friends names are Mod, Clod, Bab, Ian, Jan-Jan, Mare'k, Hairy, Shah'n and Geary. Updates on their lives are as follows:

Clod and Mod got Mary'd in M'Wacky. Clod looked nice, but Mod's outfit was body. Father Jan and Sister Ian celebrated too. Shah'n cot the flu and couldn't come wit.

Hairy got a Mohock and went out to the bares to show it ah'f. Geary dint go becoz he cot the flu. Hairy seen a nice-lookin' bra'd there, but bored her with his knotty language. He tocks endlessly like dat. He looked a little goddy, but he's pretty BRA knee since he's bin liftin' weights.

Jan-Jan liked to play chess with Bab, till he lost upon and a cass'll. Jan-Jan's dotter wanted to play, but wasn't allowed so she watched He-Ha and Mod ah'n TV.

They all went to see *Stair Wars*. It wasn't fair so they wocked over by dare. Clod didn't want to pay for all the tickets so Bab bottom. Bab's no popper, coz he tot la fur a livin'.

Translation

My friends names are Maude, Claude, Bob, Ann, John-John, Mark, Harry, Sean and Garry. Updates on their lives are as follows:

Claude and Maude got married in Milwaukee. Claude looked nice, but Maude's outfit was baudy. Father John and

Sister Ann celebrated too. Sean caught the flu and couldn't come.

Harry got a Mohawk and went to the bars to show it off. Garry didn't go because he caught the flu. Harry saw a nice-looking broad there, but bored her with his naughty language. He talks endlessly like that. He looked a little gaudy, but he's pretty brawny since he's been lifting weights.

John-John liked to play chess with Bob till he lost a pawn and a castle. John-John's daughter wanted to play, but wasn't allowed so she watched Hee-Haw and Maude on TV.

They all went to see *Star Wars*. It wasn't far so they walked there. Claude didn't want to pay for all the tickets so Bob bought them. Bob is no pauper because he taught law for a living.

Pal EYE na Paulina Street

Da Jeffer CTA 6 Jeffery Express from loop to Southside

Illinois State Circus our local government

Polish Broadway Milwaukee Avenue between Diversey and Belmont

The friendly confines Wrigley Field

DITKA . . . also known as God

The Year football flashbacks to 1985

Man Cow Daytime radio host

Damn Ryan Dan Ryan Expressway

Da Pikkaza The Picasso sculpture in Daley Plaza

The Boreman I-80—I-94 from the IL/IN state line to the Indiana Toll Road

The YIKE! I-290 (short for the Eisenhower [or Ike])

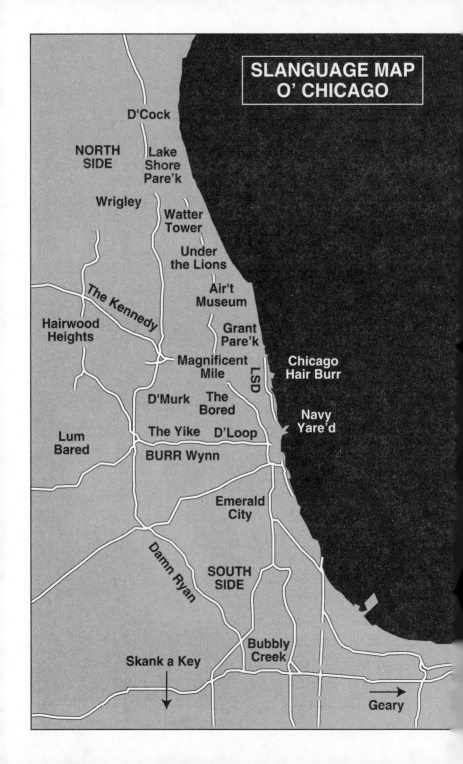

Northwest Tollway the Kennedy after it passes O'Hare Airport (I-90)

Emerald City Lower Wacker Drive

From the post office to da junction .... On traffic reports, the post office is equivalent to downtown. Da junction is up north somewhere (the Kennedy and Eden expressways split).

The green rocket or silver bullet el train

Holy Cow! words spoken in homage to the late Harry Caray

Da Coach Mike Ditka

Da cave Hubbard's tunnel on the Kennedy tollway

Gad the man upstairs

The Trib the *Chicago Tribune* newspaper

The Magnificent Mile (also called the Mag Mile): a well-known upper-class shopping district and general tourist attraction on Michigan Avenue

Under the lions the best place to meet a companion when going to the Art Institute for the day (there are two famous lion statues at the entrance)

The Outer Drive Lake Shore Drive. Only stupid out-of-towners say LSD.

When I lived in Chicago, my friends used to say "Yo Mike, go tock to those chicks with yer stupid Philly accent." My friend John Paduker also used to like to ask me, "Yo Mike. Why do they put cheese on the steak sandwiches in Philly? Does the meat stink?" My smart-ass answer: "Have the Cubs won the World Series?" All in good fun.

Overbydere over there

Bubbly Creek south fork of the south branch of the Chicago River. They used to throw the carcasses into it from the stockyards—just to add a bit of detail to that one.

Parkway little strip of grass between your sidewalk and the street

Madman's route Lower East Wacker Drive

The Bored large financial futures market where they trade pork bellies and treasury bonds. Fun place to work.

Cincinnati, Ohio

Nicknames Porkopolis, Cincy, Sin City, Cinty, Cinsinnasty, Sin sin AT a, the Natty

Most popular phrase "Come on already and forgive Pete." There are also many people known as double crossers. Not dishonest people, they are people who cross the Ohio river twice a day to and from work.

Famous local food Five-way—chili (peculiar Cincinnati blend [via Lebanon] with cinnamon, ginger and some other spices) on wet, soft, overcooked spaghetti, topped with raw onions, kidney beans, shredded cheddar cheese, and an oyster cracker.

A four-way is a five-way without the beans. Cuts down on gas.

If you're like me, you probably liked the sitcom *WKRP in Cincinnati*. Can anybody tell me what the guy is singing at the end of the show? The song has a cool tune, but I can't make out the lyrics. It's something like, "went to the bartender, bartender, went to the bar in a pockin roe star. I said, good bartender, do do do do do do doo. And a good love and a good bartender . . ." Someone please translate this song for me! Please send me an e-mail at "mike1@slanguage.com"

A four-way-bean is a five-way minus onions. This helps cut down on the bad breath.

A three-way is only for wimps. It's spaghetti, chili and cheese. You won't have any problems with gas or bad breath with this one. Still good, though.

Well-known spot The "Humming Bridge" is a suspension bridge connecting to Kentucky that actually hums as you drive across.

Popular sport/leisure We love watching the Reds and long for the days of the Big Red Machine.

MISCELLANEOUS SLANGUAGE

Proctor and God large local employer Procter & Gamble

Marge Schott and Pete Rose Reds to be forgiven

U Cats University of Cincinnati alumni

Please? What did you say?

Cheese Coney or Coney Island hot dog with chili, onions and cheese on top

Pop what you drink after you eat chili

Warsh what you do to your clothes when they get dirty

Pony Keg place to buy beer

Big Mac Bridge Cincinnati bridge that connects Cincy to Kentucky

Five-way inverted and dry Same as a five-way, but with the cheese under all that stuff, and with the chili juice drained off.

Greaters best ice cream in town

Turd Way Turfway Park Race Track

Da Clones and Da Crown the Cincinnati Cyclones and where the Cyclones play

Dolly Parton buildings the Procter & Gamble buildings

Squares city blocks

Sunken Lunken The low-lying city airport in eastern Cincy, officially named Lunken Airport

Phoney Coney hot dog bun chili, cheese, no hot dog

Little Kings uncrowned king of beer, even if it is ale

Hudey another local beer

Four corners where two streets cross

Pat & Joes where you go to get the cheep stuff

Sin-sin-AT-a how older people say "Cincinnati"

Charlie Hustle Pete Rose. Let him back in baseball.

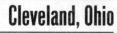

Cleveland, Ohio

Nickname Don't even call Cleveland "the mistake on the lake." You'll get hurt.

Most popular phrase "How 'bout
them Indians?" is the usual
greeting to open conversation with strangers instead
of talking about the weather.

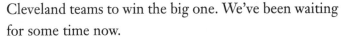

Well-known spot Da Flats is a
popular Cleveland night club/
entertainment area on the river.

Popular sport/leisure waiting for our
Cleveland teams to win the big one. We've been waiting
for some time now.

MISCELLANEOUS SLANGUAGE

The Rapid Cleveland's rail transit system

Emerald Necklace Cleveland's Metroparks system

Tree lawn strip of grass between sidewalk and street

The Jake Jacob's Field, home of the beloved Cleveland Indians

North Coast how Clevelanders refer to their location

Buzzard unofficial mascot of Cleveland; refers to popular
radio station WMMS and also the annual return of buz-
zards to Hinckley, Ohio

Forest City old Cleveland nickname for the city

Ghoulardi famous local entertainer who went on to stardom
in LA as the voice-over announcer for ABC

"Go to hell Modell" unofficial motto of the city after Art
Modell moved the football team to Baltimore

Pee Dee Cleveland's *Plain Dealer*, local paper

Pea Oh See former local beer, often called Pride of Cleveland

The Heights generic name for several of the suburbs of
Cleveland (Cleveland Heights, Maple Heights, Shaker
Heights, Garfield Heights)

Dead Man's Curve infamous stretch of I-90 near downtown;
scene of numerous car and truck crashes

The Tribe Cleveland Indians baseball team

Turney Tech nickname of former Ohio State mental institution at the intersection of Warner and Turney roads

The Dawg Pound bleachers section of the old stadium where
the most enthusiastic Browns fans used to sit.

Big Dog Browns fan that always showed up when TV focused
on the Dawg Pound. The big guy with the dog mask.

Chuckhole pothole, more common on West Side

Prospect street formerly known for its prostitutes. Usage:
"What do you want me to do for money, walk Prospect?"

Crooked River 1) the Cuyahoga River 2) beer named after
said river

Cloverleaf area surrounding the intersection of I-77 and I-480

Red-Right-88, the Drive, the Fumble, the Catch, the Shot tragic
instances in Cleveland sports history

Coventry Cleveland Heights neighborhood popular with
people who are pierced in many places

Columbus, Ohio

Nicknames Cowlumbus, Cowtown, Cols, Klums

Well-known spot 12th Street is infamous for parties that end
with police tear gas.

Popular sport/leisure We love the Buckeyes. Woody Hayes was a revered coach at OSU who had no aversion to occasionally punching the opposition in the head.

MISCELLANEOUS SLANGUAGE

The Bucks Ohio State football team

The Horseshoe Ohio Stadium

Cozy Ohio's Center of Science and Industry

The Oval OSU's huge courtyard-type place surrounded by buildings

Buckeye a person from Ohio; also a seed from a tree that many out-of-staters try to eat because they don't know it's poisonous

Old and Grungy and Scuzzy-oto Olentangy and Scioto rivers, which meet in downtown Klums

Kitty Litter Beach Alum Creek Reservoir's beach—it's as close as we can get to sand this far inland

Short North area of town just north of downtown and south of campus

All in TAN gee Olentangy River

The Schott the Schottenstein arena

Big Bear grocery store

High Street main strip—most people walking on this street are high

Cowtown the name that captures the true feel and spirit of Columbus. Often used in the alternative press.

Picktown Pickerington, Ohio (town southeast of Columbus)

The Bottoms a section of Columbus located downtown, just west of the Scioto

Corpus Christi, Texas

MISCELLANEOUS SLANGUAGE

SPID main roadway, South Padre Island Drive

Bluff rats people who live in Flour Bluff, between Corpus Christi and Padre Island. People who live here are either white trash or wealthy.

"Between the Malls" Staples Street at SPID, surrounded by Padre-Staples Mall and Sunrise Mall

West Side dangerous side of town

Southside considered safe and prosperous

Bayfront downtown

Shoreline Shoreline Drive, leading from the Bayfront to Cole Park

T-Heads popular entertainment site for locals and tourists alike

Way Out Weber the boonies

Dallas, Texas

Nickname Big D in the state of "taxes"

Most popular phrase "How 'bout dem Boys?" A reference to our beloved football team, the Cowboys.

Famous local food Shiner is the local beer of choice.

Well-known spot The "Central Distressway" is a street to be avoided if possible.

Popular sport/leisure checking out the Wowboys on a Sundee afternoon

MISCELLANEOUS SLANGUAGE

Beef Jerky dinner

Ah stay iced tea

Wowboys our football team

Coal bare cold beer

Central Distressway what we call Central Expressway 75 (aka US 75)

Wuox a HAT she city south of here that nobody can pronounce

Thuh Bubble or Thuh Park Highland Park, really nice neighborhood in Dallas

BDH Big Dallas Hair

Mix Master where I-30, I-35 and US 75 meet downtown

Denver, Colorado

Nicknames Queen City of the Plains, Dusty Old Cowtown, Mile High

Most popular phrase "Did you bag a fourteener?" This is not a reference to something perverted. It is an inquiry as to your efforts to climb any of the 14,000-foot mountains near Denver.

Famous local food Rocky Mountain Oysters, fried bulls' testicles, are a local delicacy.

Well-known spot Many enjoy going to the Big Mac (McNichols Arena) to watch the Avalanche play.

Popular sport/leisure Skiers wait all summer for the "waisties"— waist-deep powder that's a gift from God for any skier.

MISCELLANEOUS SLANGUAGE

Lo-Do lower downtown Denver
Mousetrap intersection of I-25 and I-70

Blake Street Bombers the Colorado Rockies baseball team

Orange Crush Denver Broncos defense (a little dated, but still effective)

Denver Boot large, heavy metal gizmo people find on their front tire when they don't pay their parking tickets

Two ana quarter Interstate Highway I-225

Colorado Cool-Aid Coors beer

Colorado mockingbird Burro

Denverites residents of the city and county of Denver

Dr. Cog Denver Regional Council of Governments

Cash Register that building that looks like a cash register

Yuppie-Bahn Highway C-470, where speeds (illegally) approach those of the German autobahn

Des Moines, Iowa

INTELLECTUALS OUT WANDERING AROUND

Nickname Some of the kids call it "Dud Moines" when they're bored.

Most popular phrase "Go home, picklehead."
This is a reference to our neighbors up north.

Famous local food Wandas are a popular Des Moines pastry.

Well-known spot Seni Omsed is an annual festival. The name is derived from "Des Moines" spelled backward.

MISCELLANEOUS SLANGUAGE

Cow College Iowa State University

Snooseville Scandinavian community in North Des Moines

Little Italy South Des Moines

Scoopin' the Loop cruising downtown Des Moines

RAGBRAI (pronounced RAG brye) the (Des Moines) *Register*'s Great Bicycle Ride Across Iowa

Oh ma God town across the river from Council Bluffs (Omaha)

Ioway old-timers pronounce our state this way

Juice bars topless and bottomless nudie dance bars

Worst Des Moines nickname for West Des Moines, a snooty suburb

The Absolut Building one of the psuedo-skyscrapers owned by some insurance company—the way it's designed makes it look EXACTLY like a bottle of Absolut Vodka

Detroit, Michigan

MOTOR
CITY
COBRA

Nicknames D Town, Motor City

Most popular phrase "apple knockers" or "sugar beeters," terms for people who live in lower Michigan below the Mackinac Bridge

Famous local food "poonch-keys" (paczykys), jelly doughnuts only sold on Fat Tuesday in

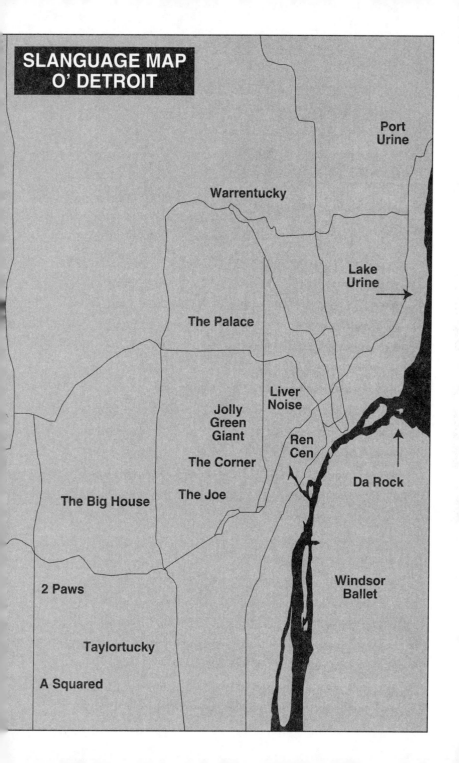

Hamtramck (pronounced Ham TRAM mick). We also eat a lot of pasties. They're meat, potatoes, and vegetables stuffed in a folded piecrust and baked.

Well-known spot The Big Mac is a sandwich and it's also the Mackinac Bridge. It joins Michigan's upper and lower peninsulas.

Popular sport/leisure We all go to the Joe to watch the Wings.

MISCELLANEOUS SLANGUAGE

Youper Michigan upper peninsula resident

Down river areas south of Metro Detroit

Greek Town popular downtown tourist area

The Corner Tiger Stadium

Grash it Gratiot Avenue

Liver noise Livernois

Lasher Lahser

Freep *Detroit Free Press*

Lowper Youper term for a resident of lower pennisula

Boston cooler milkshake made of Vernor's and vanilla ice cream

Ren Cen Renaissance Center

Vernor's ginger ale

Fudgies people who vacation in Michigan's upper peninsula who traditionally buy Mackinac Island Fudge

Jolly Green Giant statue "Spirit of Detroit" located in downtown Detroit adjacent to the west wall of the City-County Building.

E-way what in the rest of the U.S. is called a freeway

Two Paws nearby town of Paw Paw, Michigan

Banana belt nickname for Escanaba, Michigan, because of its mild winters.

Eugene, Oregon

Nicknames You JEAN is the correct pronunciation of our fair city. We're also called the Emerald City.

Most popular phrase "Quack" expresses the fact that you are a Duck fan.

Well-known spot Yachats (Yah Hots) is a resort community on the coast, with a sign saying, "Welcome to Yachats," placed exactly where you can't see it—thereby ensuring you will drive past it.

Popular sport/leisure Surfin' the Pass is practiced by snowboarders at the Willamette Pass ski area.

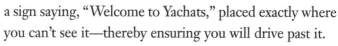

MISCELLANEOUS SLANGUAGE

Gang Green University of Oregon Ducks fans

Webfoot University of Oregon Ducks fan

Duck University football team fan (which is everyone, or you lie and say you are to save your life)

Webfeet what we are born with here, because we are Ducks and it rains all the time

> The WOW Hall is sort of a counterculture gathering place for those who enjoy loud music while dancing like zombies. Previously it was the Woodsmen of the World.

Fredy's Fred Meyer store, our favorite everything store

OR a gun our state of being. There really IS a huge state in between San Francisco and Seattle. HONEST!

Will AAH mit a river runs through us

WILL uh mit obvious tourist (sigh)

Draggin' the Gut now outlawed (see sign) teen practice of slowly driving their cars up and down Willamette Street on Friday night and shouting lewd suggestions at prospective love interests

Loggers extinct species of previously employed persons, the descendants of whom all now work for Hyundai and wear little sterile suits and baggies over their beards

Drain, Fossil, Boring nearby city names

Cherry Poppin' Daddies popular local bar band

Gainesville, Florida

Nicknames G-ville, Hogtown

Most popular phrase "North until you smell it, west until you step in it" are the directions to Tallahassee from Gainesville.

Well-known spot "Chinee-takee-
outee"—Best Chinese food
in town (that really is the
name of the restaurant).

MISCELLANEOUS SLANGUAGE

The Spice Carribean Spice Restaurant
Nard's Leonardo's by the slice
The Rotator J.D. Penguins on North 441
The Porp the Purple Porpoise, a popular bar
"Live a life with porpoise" Drink at the Porpoise all the time.
Santa Play Santa Fe Community College
The Prairie Paines Prairie Wildlife Reserve
The O'Dome the Stephen C. O'Connell Center on campus
Lacksity Lake City (located north on I-75)

Gettysburg, Pennsylvania

Nickname Guess Burr
Most popular phrase "Where was
Pickett's charge?"
Well-known spot The "square" is the
circle in the middle of town.
Popular sport/leisure Watching the
"tursts" come through town
keeps us busy all summer long.

MISCELLANEOUS SLANGUAGE

Arntsvl The National Apple Harvest Festival is located just north of Arntsvl.

Bigerbill The Bigerbill Road goes north outta town.

He's gone t' the Woo He went to Wooster College.

Gloucester, Massachussetts

Updaline up the line, referring to any of the malls or restaraunts found if you follow route 128 south toward Boston

The Fish Tank our local hockey rink, home of the Gloucester High School Fishermen

Bullavahd Stacey Boulevard, perennial hangout for local teens

Glosta local pronounciation of "Gloucester"

Wohf all of the docks that together comprise the seaport of Gloucester

Wingahsheek beach and surrounding affluent neighborhood in West Gloucester

The Fort Commercial Street and St. Peter's Square area, host of annual Fiesta

Ten Pound Island small island situated in middle of Gloucester Harbor, alleged to be infested with rats

Danvis also known as Danvers, hated rivals in high school sports

The Cut officially called the Blymnan Bridge, it is a small man-made waterway that separates Gloucester from the mainland

Back Shuh naturally beautiful area of East Gloucester, home to summer residents and motels

Honolulu, Hawaii

Most popular phrase Remember that "Ma Hollow" means thank you. People see it on the trash cans and think it means trash.

Famous local food Pupus are appetizers that don't taste like the word sounds.

Well-known spot Don't miss Da Keys if you visit Hawaii (Waikiki).

Popular sport/leisure We go anywhere the surf is macking.

MISCELLANEOUS SLANGUAGE

Taxed mugged
Bumby later
Da kine OK
Shakas Hi

"Shakas, da kine bumby, choke grinds." This is local speak for hello, all right buddy, good food. Be forewarned: Some of the natives might hurt you if you try to talk like them.

Vog volcano haze

You come eat my house a dinner invitation

Crack seed preserved flavored fruit, usually plums

Choke nuts a rather wacky situation

Small kine just a little bit

Onolicious delicious (Hawaiian style)

Shootz brah, I like grind awready Enough bro, I want to eat now

Chop suey all mixed up

Who who to be angry

Get choke people, bra! There's a lot of people, dude!

Shaka! What's up?

You go stay go, I go stay come. You go on ahead, and I will come later.

If can, can. If no can, no can. If you are able to, then you will. If you are not able to, then you won't.

He stay all salty. He is rather upset.

Shootz, bra! It's macking! Wow, man! The surf is up!

Walk yo' jaws. Leave me alone.

No scade brah. Don't be afraid, brother, or No fear, man.

Da Keys Waikiki

Eh, brah, like grind? Do you want to go eat?

Broke da mouth refers to any food that is excellent

Houston, Texas

Nicknames H Town, Clutch City

Most popular phrases "Heidi Do, y'all," is a common greeting among locals. "Gimme a Coke" might get you a Coke, Sprite or Dr Pepper.

Well-known spot the Dome, where the Stros play

Popular sport/leisure hangin' at the Chocolate buy you

MISCELLANEOUS SLANGUAGE

Yous Ton Houston

Skeeter hawks dragonflies

Heidi Houston greeting

Hell season experienced in Houston from July to September

Big Sam Big Sam Houston, the man our town was named after

The South-Worst Freeway Highway 59, site of major traffic jams

Dalitude what Houstonians get from Dallasites

Coke any carbonated beverage, regardless of color, flavor or brand

Yankee anyone from north of Oklahoma

Gunnies Gunnie's Shack, popular bar near or in Spring, Texas, hence the term "Gunnie run"

The Laptop or the Desktop Compaq Center, where the Rockets play

The Stros our baseball team

Chocolate buy you brown river of mud (and other things) we canoe in

Indianapolis, Indiana

Nicknames Nap Town, Circle City

Most popular phrase "I have to admit I'm a HEAD" (Hoosiers Embarassed About Dan Quayle).

Famous local food When you want a canteloupe, ask for a musk melon or mush melon.

Well-known spot SoBro, a popular, artsy neighborhood in Broad Ripple Village. The name is modeled after NYC's SoHo, which means "south of Houston Street."

Popular sport/leisure Watching the Five Hunnert is the best thing going here.

MISCELLANEOUS SLANGUAGE

Five Hunnert Indianapolis 500

Tara Hut Terra Haute

Hoshians Terre Haute natives

India-no-place our city when it annoys or bores us

Ooey-Pooey IUPUI, local university (Indiana University—Purdue University at Indianapolis)

MSA Market Square Arena, where the Pacers play

The General Bobby Knight (coined by Dick Vitale)

The Dome place where the Colts play

The Fascist mall mall at Keystone at the Crossing officially known as the fashion mall.

The Track Indianapolis Motor Speedway

Jacksonville, Florida

Nicknames Jax, Actionville

Well-known spot Big BM is the Baptist Medical Center, the largest in the region.

Popular sport/leisure We love our Jag Wires football team.

MISCELLANEOUS SLANGUAGE

Or TEA Guh Ortega

PV Ponte Vedra or Palm Valley

When visiting Jacksonville, don't be concerned if your friends keep mentioning big BM's and little BM's. They're not constipated, they're merely discussing the nicknames of some of the local medical centers.

Jackson Vuhl our city
Lizard Kings local East Coast Hockey League team
JTB J. Turner Butler Boulevard
Cecil Naval air station Cecil Field
NAS or NAS JAX Jacksonville Naval Air Station
The Planet happening radio station in Jacksonville
Homerdome First Baptist Church, led by Homer Lindsay Jr.,
    the largest church in Jacksonville and one of the largest
    in the United States
The Beach anything east of the ditch (Intercoastal Waterway)
The U University Medical Center
Little BM by the Sea Baptist Medical Center–Beaches, affili-
    ated with the much larger Baptist Medical Center
Times-Onion *Times-Union*, our largest local newspaper
Tee you *Florida Times Union* newspaper
WD Winn-Dixie (large southern grocery store chain)
Jax Navy nickname for a credit union in Jacksonville

Kansas City, Missouri

Nicknames Can City, BBQ Capital, Home
    of Jazz, Kay See Em Oh, City of
    Fountains, Kay See Moe
Most popular phrase "How come you
    don't have an accent?"
Famous local food We are the barbe-
    cue capital of the world.

Well-known spot We call the Missouri River the Big Muddy. It's too thin to plow, too thick to drink.

Popular sport/leisure The I-70 Series, the 1985 World Series between the St. Louis Cardinals and the KC Royals. It was the best—akin to a subway series in NYC without having to go there.

MISCELLANEOUS SLANGUAGE

Darth Vader Building big, black, looming office building in JoCo

Saint Joe a city to the north (St. Joseph)

KCK (Kay See Kay) Kansas City

The K nickname for Kauffman Stadium used by the media, hated by most of the locals

Flush Creek Brush Creek, which runs through the Plaza and has been found to be contaminated with sewage

Electric Haircurlers "sculptures" on top of the convention center (Bartle Hall)

Mighty Moe Missouri River (when we're feeling nice about it)

Jeff City Jefferson City, the Missouri state capital

Peculiarites people who live in Peculiar

Red pop soda served only at Gate's BBQ, as in the phrase "Yew wan red pop wi' that?"

The Quiz Dan Quisenberry, former KC Royals pitcher

Under the 12th Street bridge never go there unless you have 50 people with you

Killem Park local park known for its high body count

Suicide Hill best local sledding hill, Brookside Park

Kennedy Space Center, Florida

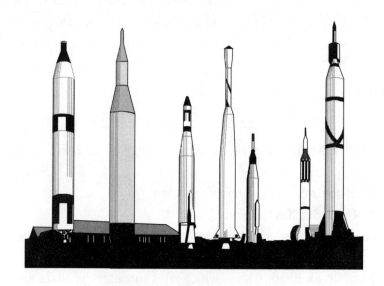

MISCELLANEOUS SLANGUAGE

Rocket Ranch Kennedy Space Center
Gray Beard long-term, wise employee
Pad Rat worker at the launch site
Bus driver astronaut
Dinney Worl East Kennedy Space Center
Blue suiter Air Force launch team member

Ketchikan, Alaska

MISCELLANEOUS SLANGUAGE

Ketchikan Sneakers red rubber
boots

Web Feet what many
people in Ketchi-
kan grow

Cheechako
someone
who is
new here
(possibly
from the word "Chicago")

Skiff small open boat, from Norway

Skookum solidly built

Endo turn something end for end

Ketchikanites who we are

PPPs Pink Polyester Pantsuits, as worn by old lady tourists

Turistas name for the 500,000 tourists who visit here each
summer, also called cattle or lemmings

Lutefisk smelly cod preserved in lye, a Norwegian delicacy

Halibut jacket gray wool jacket, standard fare

Ketchikan suitcase overpacked and duct-taped cardboard box

Kirksville, Missouri

MISCELLANEOUS SLANGUAGE

Kirks, Kirkatoids what the college students call the townies

Da S*itty a favorite after-party hangout

Da Lake Thousand Hills State Park

Yankees what students from south of St. Louis call students from north of St. Louis

St. Looser what students from Chicago call students from Missouri

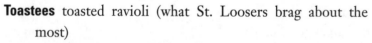

Toastees toasted ravioli (what St. Loosers brag about the most)

Husker someone from Nebraysker

Shruman State what the stoners call Truman State University

Da potato an oblong crack in one of the sidewalks, supposedly bad luck to walk on—as in, "Step on a crack, break your mother's back." Only freshmen walk on it.

63 best way to leave Kirksville

SoCo South County area of St. Louis

Knoxville, Tennessee

Nickname Nocks Vull, Nogzvull

Most popular phrase "Go Vols" is heard during football season. It's short for "Go Volunteers."

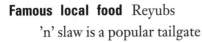

Famous local food Reyubs 'n' slaw is a popular tailgate food.

Well-known spot "The Strip," aka Cumbarland Avenue

Popular sport/leisure We don't like the Crimson Tide. You might hear "Buck Fama" here and there.

MISCELLANEOUS SLANGUAGE

Yane firm ran hare Welcome to the area.

Murr Vull neighboring city of Maryville

Whistle Pig Tennessee name for the groundhog

Forks over the branches a bridge

Gater hater Tennessee fan

Buck Fama popular slander for our Crimson Tide counterparts

Reelin spurrier fishin'

Lancaster, Pennsylvania

Nickname The locals say LANK a stir. Out-of-towners say Lang CAST er.

Most popular phrase "Vee live in Pencil WAYNE ya."

Famous local food Schnitts and knepp is Pennsylvania Dutch for apples and ham. Any Amish smorgasborg with heavy, fatty foods is very popular with the tourists and fat people alike.

Well-known spot Tourists love to visit the nearby towns of Paradise, Intercourse and Blue Balls.

Popular sport/leisure Many people come here to shop at the OTT-lets. Outlets are stores with sometimes cheaper prices for clothes, gifts, etc.

MISCELLANEOUS SLANGUAGE

Taste like more delicious
Wickter, your off is all. Victor, your vacation is over.
Hooftee ghost
The baby's grexy The baby's cranky.
Mishty Amish person
Flossy an Amish woman in a dress
The best way to Paradise is through Intercourse (the route between New Holland and Paradise, Pennsylvania).

Two flossies, Sadie and Rachel, were pickin' potatoes, discussing their husbands, Jakie and Abner. Upon harvesting two huge potatoes, Sadie remarked, "Look Rachel, they're just like my Jakie's." "Why, because they're so big?" asked Rachel. "No," answered Sadie. "Because they're so dirty."

Dutchified the way we speak here in Pennsylvania Dutch Country

I sit wide, ain't? I take up a lot of room when I sit down, isn't that so?

Las Vegas, Nevada

Nickname Lost Wages

Famous local food

Get yourself a rib-sticking, all-you-can-eat smorgasborg for only a dollar ninety-nine!

Well-known spot

Anywhere in Lost Wages can be called an adult Disneyland.

Popular sport/leisure You can get married and divorced here as often as you like.

MISCELLANEOUS SLANGUAGE

D.I. short for Desert Inn (road and hotel)

Trop short for Tropicana (street and hotel)

T.I. Treasure Island (hotel)

State bird crane (building crane)

Five points where Charleston Boulevard, Boulder Highway, Fremont Street, Easter and what used to be called 25th Street (now also Easter) meet

The Strip Las Vegas Boulevard

Loose describes a slot machine that pays often

Fleas dealer's slang for low-limit grind bettors that just won't go away

T & M Thomas and Mack Center, where UNLV basketball games are played

The Shoe the Horseshoe Casino downtown

TAM card what every bartender in Las Vegas must be familiar with before tending bar—Techniques of Alcohol Management

Juice got connections for work or play

R.J. the *Las Vegas Review-Journal*

The Shark Tank Thomas and Mack Arena, where the Runnin' Rebels play basketball

Squeezers Palace slang for Caesars Palace hotel

Wingnuts guys from Nellis Air Force base, north of Las Vegas

Hump to Pahrump a mountain pass leading to the town of Pahrump, west of Las Vegas

OK Highway Oran K. Gragson Highway (section of I-95 that cuts through the center of town)

Pay attention to what the dealers and casino employees are saying about you. Sometimes they're complimenting you. Sometimes they ain't.

A George is a patron who tips well.

A Larry is a poor tipper.

A shill is someone who is paid to play a game by the casino, hopefully drawing other customers.

Fleas are what dealers call low-limit bettors who won't go away.

A whale is a high roller who is given all the comps: free room, booze, jet ride, etc.

Pitboss the supervisor of a "pit" of tables, e.g., dice pit, 21 pit, etc.

Jackpot a mess of trouble

Sing to call a long sequence of winning dice rolls

Stroak to purposefully place a complicated bet to annoy the dealer

Bird 25 cents (usually)

Nickel five dollars

Dime ten dollars

Tokes tips

Color to convert odd denominational winnings into an easy-to-manage handful

DICE SLANG

Midnight twelve

Boxcars twelve

Snake eyes two
C and E crap and eleven
Hardways when the dice are identical (two ones, two twos, etc.)

Little Rock, Arkansas

Nickname Li'l Raw'k
Most popular phrase SUUUUUUEEEEE WEEEE is the female razorback.
Famous local food We love Chicken Stick. It's a chicken breast on a corn dog stick.
Well-known spot North Little Rock, aka Dog Town. Supposedly, stray dogs caught in Little Rock are dumped here.
Popular sport/leisure Y'all can spend lots of time turtle poppin' here. That's shooting turtles in the bayou with a shotgun from the bank.

MISCELLANEOUS SLANGUAGE

Pine Tree Tech University of Arkansas–Little Rock (UALR)
University of Arkansas Last Resort UALR
Dog Town North Little Rock, across the river, supposedly where stray dogs caught in Little Rock are dumped
The Pig Trail the dangerous scenic route carved into the Ozarks leading to Fayetteville

Dicksonites people who hang out on Dickson Street, a popular entertainment strip

Pyoolaskey County Little Rock's pronunciation of the name of its county, Pulaski

Los Angeles, California

Nicknames Smell A, Hell A, Behind the Orange Curtain, Los Scandalous, Los San Diegeles, LaLa Land, Ill A, City of Angels

HOLLY WEIRD

Most popular phrase "My Laxaphobia is acting up." Laxaphobia is fear of Los Angeles International Airport (LAX is the airport symbol).

Famous local food Start your morning with a Chino. It's short for cappucino.

Popular sport/leisure You might find yourself chillin' at the tilt. This is a reference to relaxing at home after the earthquake of 1994, which left many houses askew.

MISCELLANEOUS SLANGUAGE

The Boo or Big Boo Malibu, to locals

Sig Alert traffic jam or when the highway patrol closes the freeway because of an accident

Smaze smoke and haze (better than smog)

Earthquake weather unseasonably hot

Go Wood going Hollywood in attitude

The Hills rich areas of Southern California

Orange Crush intersection of Interstate 5 with I-22 and I-57

PCH Pacific Coast Highway

The Five Interstate 5

Berdoo San Bernadino, to locals

Laxaphobia fear of Los Angeles International Airport (LAX)

Slimy Valley Simi Valley

Behind the orange curtain living in Orange County

Kraproom Moorpark spelled backward

Saint Freakshow what we from LA call Frisco

Los San Diegeles the section of uninterrupted coastal development from LA to San Diego

Mausoleum the Coliseum, where USC football is played

Old Pas trendy area of Pasadena to shop and hang out

The Valley San Fernando Valley

So Cal huge metropolitan area encompassing LA, OC, and outlying areas

The Strand bike path along the beach in South Bay area of LA

S & M Boulevard Santa Monica Boulevard

WeHo West Hollywood

NoHo North Hollywood

Over the hill in the San Fernando Valley, speaking from the LA basin

The Strip the famous Sunset Strip

BevCen The Beverly Center, an upscale shopping mall near Beverly Hills frequently seen on *90210*

Hollyweird Hollywood

BH Beverly Hills—we rarely say "Beverly Hills"

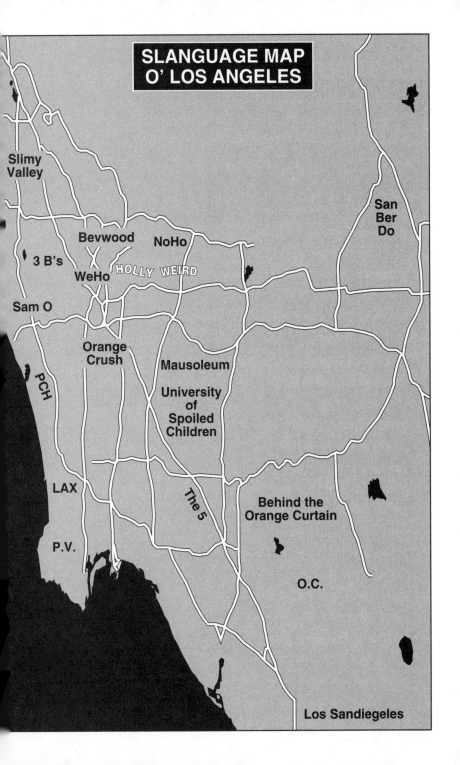

House of Schmooze House of Blues

Angelinos what we call ourselves

The OTHER valley refers to the San Gabriel Valley

Inland Empire area in So Cal also known as the Valley. Includes such cities as San Bernardino, Riverside, Rialto, Fontana, Colton, Loma Linda, Redlands, Highland and Yucaipa, and is almost completely surrounded by mountains.

Wastewood Westwood

Smellsegundo El Segundo (huge sewage treatment plant there)

Garbage Grove freeway Garden Grove freeway

Four-level where four freeways intersect in downtown LA

USC university of spoiled children

HB Huntington Beach

MAW model, actress, whatever

Louisville, Kentucky

Nicknames Loo Ah Vull, Loonyville, Derby City

Most popular phrase "Dubby Day's coming soon."

Famous local food Derby pie is a chocolate and pecan pie served at the Kentucky Derby. We also love frickled (fried) pickles.

Well-known spot You can't go wrong at the Kentucky Derby, Churchill Downs or the Kentucky Oaks. Even if you don't like horses, you can gamble on them to pass the time.

Popular sport/leisure You gotta admit, the women here got cute accents. It's fun just to sit and listen to them.

MISCELLANEOUS SLANGUAGE

Dubby Day day of the Kentucky Derby

Sweettea tea with sugar already in it; standard tea in restaurants

The Waterson I-264

C-J The *Louisville Courier-Journal*

The Oaks the Kentucky Oaks, a race for three-year-old fillies

The Downs Churchill Downs

Dixie Die-Way once-gruesome portion of Dixie Highway

The Loop little shops area where Douglass, Bardstown, and Dundee meet

Olop Our Lady of Peace (sanitarium)

Yoo-vel U of L, the University of Louisville

Derby Pie tasty (and patented) pie of pecans and chocolate

Not everybody in America is anti-smoking. Especially if y'all are a backy farmer. Here's an excellent local credo: All hail the King Tobbaco! May his money and cancer rain down upon us forever!

Louisville Lip Muhammad Ali, aguably the greatest boxer of all time (after Philadelphia's Joe Frazier, of course), was called this when he lived here as Cassius Clay

Kentuckiana what we call the entire Northern Kentucky/ Southern Indiana region

WAVE Country what one of the local TV stations (WAVE) calls the entire region

Memphis, Tennessee

Nicknames Miffus, Birthplace of the Blues

Most popular phrase "Sweet or unsweet?" You'll be asked this when you order iced tea.

Famous local food Be sure to order "a white, pulled, hot and grazed" when you visit here. You'll get a chunky barbeque with cole slaw and sauce.

Well-known spot Birthplace of the Blues is the famous Beale Street in Memphis.

Popular sport/leisure Just hanging out playing the blues keeps everybody happy here.

MISCELLANEOUS SLANGUAGE

Out East the suburbs east of Memphis

Memphibians folks from Memphis

Devils East Memphis residents

Cooper–Young small historical district with decent nightlife

Th' Strip Highland Avenue

Pay-Glee Way-Glee (Piggly Wiggly) Would you believe it's a grocery store?

Caught'n still grows east of the city

Death Week Elvis Presley International Tribute Week

Miami, Florida

Nicknames My Jammy, The Magic City, Me AH Me

Most popular phrase "House looks like Andrew hit it." This refers to the category 5 hurricane that hit here in 1995.

Famous local food Café Cubano— java espresso in a tiny cup with a big punch.

Well-known spot Everybody who is anybody has to be seen at SEW Bee. Say "South Beach" and you're branded a tourist.

Popular sport/leisure "Go Fish" is the cheer for the Miami Dolphins.

MISCELLANEOUS SLANGUAGE

Dah Grove Coconut Grove

Rocket Ranch Kennedy Space Center

> Floribbean is a local cuisine with elements of Floridian and Caribbean dishes. Spanglish is unofficial everyday language. The Haitian Station is where you buy beer and cigarettes. You might respond "Yes, See" as a courtesy to the Spanish population and "See, Yes" as a courtesy to the English-speaking folks.

Rattlesnake killer off-course missile that explodes in woods

Crusing the Bee checking out the nightlife in South Beach

So Fee the area south of Fifth Street in South Beach

95 Bactuptadagoldenglaydz everyday situation on I-95

Da Beach islands east of da mainland

Da Mainland area west of da Inn Ra Coastal

Da Inn Ra Coastal Intracoastal Waterway

Da Key Key Biscayne

Da Gables Coral Gables

NMB North Miami Beach

Da Trail Tamiami Trail (southwest 8th Street)

CAP Cuban-American Princess, a Cuban female yuppie

Miami natives group of people believed to be extinct, or at least endangered—everyone here is from somewhere else

Spanglish unofficial everyday language

Cortadito Cuban coffee with a dash of milk

The Conch (conk) Republic Key West and the Florida Keys

Conchs (conks) Florida Keys natives—an endangered species

Haitian Station where you buy beer and cigarettes

Milwaukee, Wisconsin

Nicknames M'Wacky, Brew City, Maukee, Mocky, Behind the Cheddar Curtain

Most popular phrase "The Pack is back" refers to our powerhouse football team, the Packers.

Famous local food Beer, cheese and beef are the three Wisconsin food groups.

Well-known spot A visit to Milwaukee isn't complete without a stop at Kopps, the world's greatest custard stand.

Popular sport/leisure We worship Brett Favre as God every day of the week during the football season.

MISCELLANEOUS SLANGUAGE

Mud ducks people from Minnesota

Bubbler water fountain

Beer depot where you buy beer

White soda 7Up or any clear drink

Brandy and Sweet awful cocktail of brandy and white soda

Cheesehead Wisconsinite

Brot heavily consumed smoked sausage

Tight on ya street named Teutonia

Let's go by Baba's Let's go to Grandma's.

Scon Sin our state

KK what everyone calls Kinnickinnic Avenue, a street that
    runs north-south through the city

Brew City a nickname for our city and our stadium

The Valley the major industrial area just south of downtown

Sudsey Milwaukee beer

Mold Style another local beer

Milwaukee City Limits where the streetcar bends the corner
    round

Schnecks local bakery products

Cousin's place to get sub sandwiches

Miller Valley our fragrant yeast

Blatz very cheap beer, sound you make when you drink it

The Beast (aka Milwaukee's Best) another beer

Polish Moon Allen-Bradly clocktower

Road to Hell Lincoln-Memorial High-Rise Bridge, now leads
    to Cudahy

Kohl's (referring to almost any food store) a food store

Mistake in your three Wisconsin food groups. It's "beer, cheese
    and brots."

Brewers Hill a few blocks of homes in the center of Mil-
    waukee

Pigsville underground community and former pig farm area
    just outside of the metro area.

Madtown our state's capitol, Madison

Paddle pop ice cream bar

"Hey dare whatcha know dare chedderhead?" Friendly
greeting heard throughout and beyond the cheddar curtain.

Kringle local flat danish pastry, formed in a ring, stuffed with fillings such as fruit, nuts and cheese, and topped with white icing

The Viaduct Southside bridge

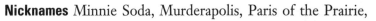

Minneapolis, Minnesota

Nicknames Minnie Soda, Murderapolis, Paris of the Prairie, Twin Cities, Minnehaha, The Cleanest City in America

Most popular phrase "Oof dah" is a Scandinavian exclamation you'll hear often in this town.

Famous local food Lutefisk is a Scandinavian delicacy. It's dried cod, rehydrated with lye. Many here think it's not even good enough for dog food.

Well-known spot All the buildings are connected by sky-walks. This keeps you warm and toasty during the harsh winter months here.

Popular sport/leisure For some unknown reason, we play Duck, Duck, Gray Duck instead of Duck, Duck, Goose.

Easiest way to label yourself a tourist Ask someone, "Where's Mary Tyler Moore's house?"

MISCELLANEOUS SLANGUAGE

Minnie Soda Minnesota correctly pronounced

Twinkies our beloved baseball team

Twin Cities preferred name for Minneapolis–St. Paul

St. Paulites inhabitants of St. Paul

Minneapaulitans people who live in St. Paul or Minneapolis

Minnie Apple Minneapolis

No Stars former hockey team

Skywalk elevated passageway between buildings

Ish! or Ishy yucky

Goofers what we call our U of M football team, the Gophers

The Twin Zits the Twin Cities

Ish Da Minnesota-speak for "a little worse than Oof Da"

Seven Corners seven-way intersection on Washington
    Avenue

Hot dish casserole

The Body our governor, Jesse "The Body" Ventura

St. Francis Fran Tarkenton, former Vikings quarterback and
    local hero

Twin Tones the Twin Cities

Doan tone downtown

Scandahoovians Scandinavians

Minnetonka city where Tonka trucks are from. I believe that
    many people refer to that city as just "Tonka."

Frogtown French-settled area of St. Paul

Pronto Pups what the rest of the country would call corn
    dogs

Barz brownies

Modesto, California

MISCELLANEOUS SLANGUAGE

Mo-town our town, Modesto

The City San Francisco

Turdlock Turlock, a town just to the south

Turkey Tech California State University, Stanislaus in Turlock. The area is known for its turkey farms.

Way out McHenry refers to a location on McHenry Avenue that is almost out of Modesto and into the country.

Five Corners/Five Points intersection of five roads in downtown Modesto

Mojave, California

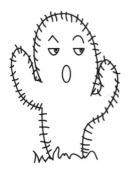

Life Line Interstate 395

Tronian one who lives by the sulfur plants

Soapfolk people who live in Boron, California

Blue-Suiter Air Force people

Ayee Vee Antelope Valley

Lope Vall also Antelope Valley
Cantelope Valley once again, Antelope Valley
Lanxster Lancaster, California
Eddy Air Patch Edwards Air Force Base, California
San Berdoo San Bernardino, California
Rosemn Rosamond, California
D Valley Death Valley
The Gay Area "Bay" Area of Cali
El Ayee Los Angeles
Graffiti "Someone from LA has been here."

Nashville, Tennessee

Nicknames Nash Vegas, Music City, Nashburg, The Third Coast

Most popular phrase "You seen that Diesel sniffer?" This refers to certain country music fans who follow their idols' buses from town to town

"The Third Coast" is a nickname for our city, due to the music writing/publishing/recording business.

Famous local food meat n' thray (most restaurants serve a slab of flesh and three side dishes)

Well-known spot Music Row is the neighborhood where most of the recording studios and record companies are located. This term also denotes the entire Nashville music industry.

Popular sport/leisure If you see the pickin', you're hearing some music.

MISCELLANEOUS SLANGUAGE

Boo Lee Vard wide traffic throughfare

See the pickin' hear some music

Vandyland area surrounding Vanderbilt University

Graceland Memphis, Tennessee

Nunbun sticky bun created by a local coffee shop just in time for the Christmas season. It put Nashville in the spotlight of the tabloids because it was said to resemble Mother Teresa.

Batman Building Nashville's sole true skyscraper

Wide loada a Wynonna Judd–size hamburger

Vanderbubble refers to the isolation/protection of Vanderbilt University from Nashville in general, also from "real life." Probably originates from "living in a bubble."

Shoppry Land mega-shopping mall under construction on the site of the closed Opryland amusement park

Sweet tea very sugary iced tea enjoyed by the locals

Unsweet tea ordinary iced tea

The Pantry the famous Pancake Pantry, where you can occasionally sight Garth Brooks. Yummy! The line to get in is as long as for Space Mountain.

The Loop the perimeter of Vanderbilt around which sorority girls jog. Once you cross inside, you're in the Vander-bubble.

Second 2nd Avenue, area downtown (very near the Batman Building) where there are a lot of fun bars

Moon pies, RC Cola and a bug zapper Friday night entertainment

Tow Motor forklift

Garth all the tourists who come here and buy cowboy boots and big hats to try to be cool

New Orleans, Louisiana

Nicknames Gnaw Lynn's, Big Easy

Most popular phrase "Throw me something, mister." You'll hear this along the parade routes at Mardi Gras. Usually the men in the parade throw trinkets or silver dimes. Nowadays, there is no silver in the dimes, though.

Famous local food Don't forget to order an Erster Po'boy dressed. It's an oyster sandwich w/lettuce, tomato and mayonnaise.

> While most cities have fall, winter, spring and summer, we in Gnaw Lynn's have our own four seasons: crab, shrimp, crawfish and king cake.

Well-known spot Two Jacks is a famous local restaurant. It is spelled Tujague, but nobody can pronounce it correctly.

Popular sport/leisure When you eat yo' crayfish, remember to pinch the heads and suck the tails, y'all.

MISCELLANEOUS SLANGUAGE

Banquette sidewalk

Neutral ground street median

Muffaletta Italian-style sandwich

Crawfish, crawdads, mudbugs different ways to say "crayfish"

Donna buy ya down at the Bayou

Life is a bowl of gumbo a jumbled mixture

Gallery streetside-facing porch

Camp Street thermos French Quarter liquor bottle holder

Who dats Saints fans

Esplanades men's undershirt

Hand grenades Everyone in the Quarter knows about these drinks. They have the same effect on your body as the real thing.

Lundy Gras day before Mardi Gras

Cha-u-tey Charity Hospital

Redbins the standard Monday meal: red beans and rice

Cookin' Earl one of the most important ingredients in fryin' catfish

Go dip up Go serve yourself.

New York, New York

Nicknames N'Yawk, Big Apple, Center of the Univoice

Most popular phrase "Oh Moy Gawd" is an exclamation for any situation. Another popular phrase that originated here is "Fugedaboudit" (forget about it).

Famous local food New Yawkas swear by egg creams. They're seltzer, chocolate syrup and milk.

Well-known spot People in New York wait *on* line, not *in* line.

Popular sport/leisure We worship the Yankees. Any questions?

MISCELLANEOUS SLANGUAGE

Pawno actors who take off their clothes and have sex

NEIGH biz they live next door to you, but you might not know them

Da Bronze a New York City borough

NoHo neighborhood north of Houston Street

SoHo neighborhood south of Houston Street

Mob'll roy marble rye (type of bread)

Soar past tense of see

Draw put your socks in it

Drawer to create a picture as art

Joy'k jerk

Whaddya whaddya? I am dumbfounded by your audacity.

TriBeCa triangular neighborhood below Canal Street

Silicone Alley the Flatiron District, with many multimedia startup companies

Oner Niner take the one or nine train downtown

Brownie a person who tickets your car

Stat Nigh Lynn Staten Island

Yonkiz and Yonkuz folks from Yonkers

Cawna Fish Treat corner of 5th Street

Bee Cue We Brooklyn Queens Expressway

L-Eye-E Long Island Expressway

Gee Dub George Washington Bridge

Da Iron Horse New York City trains

Broken Barry Tull Brooklyn Battery Tunnel

Chester draws a chest of drawers

Gorilla building Empire State Building

Dem bums before 1955, the nickname of the Brooklyn Dodgers

Dis iz de tree to de bush This is the number three express train to Flatbush Avenue.

I received my only death threat in my life via an anonymous e-mail from my New York City slanguage web page. "If you ever talk like this in New York, we'll kill you."

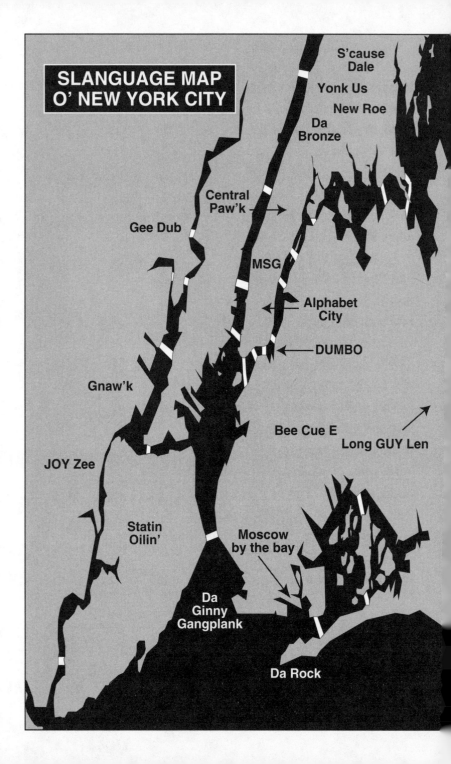

DUMBO (acronym for Down Under Manhattan Bridge Overpass) an artists community on the East River near downtown Brooklyn

Johnny pump fire hydrant

Junior's makes the best cheesecake in the world, located in downtown Brooklyn

Pal Calling someone "Pal" is not a good thing in New York.

Go to Jersey an insult

Oh moy Gawd! what most people say after they ride in a NYC taxi

Straphangers New York City subway riders

Alphabet City sketchy area east of 1st Avenue where the avenues are denoted by letters instead of numbers (e.g., Avenue A, Avenue B, etc.)

A walk on the Broad a stroll down Broadway

Barry Battery Park, Manhattan

Willie B Williamsburg Bridge

Da Ginny Gangplank Verrazano Narrows Bridge

Slow Bombs the Schloebahms Housing Projects in Yonkers

Disaster Place "This is Astor Place" (subway announcer mispronunciation)

Boat people Staten Islanders

The Mets baseball team

Bronx Bombers other baseball team

Fashion Avenue 7th Avenue in Manhattan

Moscow by the Bay Brighton Beach, the predominantly Soviet section of Coney Island in Brooklyn

Butcher Shop what residents of Brooklyn call Coney Island Hospital

Norfolk, Virginia

Squids Navy people (we have lots, we have the largest Navy base)

ERF the Elizabeth River ferry, basic transportation to Potesmeth

Potesmeth Portsmouth, the city across the river from No Fck

TRT our pathetic attempt at a mass transportation system (buses and trolleys)

BBT Bay Bridge Tunnel (avoid at all costs)

HRBT Hampton Roads Bridge Tunnel (avoid when possible)

DTT Downtown Tunnel, a good alternative to the MTT

MTT Midtown Tunnel, always backed up (avoid when possible)

Norfolkeese what we speak

Lizzy the Elizabeth River, which runs scenically through downtown and bears the dubious distinction of being the sixth most polluted in the world

Willeys-B Williamsburg, a nearby authentically colonial town featuring people wearing authentically uncomfortable colonial clothing and making candles and crap

Merry the Monitor-Merrimac Bridge Tunnel on I-664, across the James River

Honker traffic delay (as in, "Route 44 is all honkered up")

The Todds the Tides, Norfolk's AAA minor-league baseball team

Ads the Admirals, the much-loved ECHL hockey team

North Jersey
(NOT to be confused with
New York City or South Jersey)

Nicknames JAW zee or New Jaw'z

Most popular phrase "What exit ya from?" People from Jersey do hate this question, though.

Famous local food Jaw zee tomatoes

Well-known spot There are a lot of beaches here. They're referred to as "donna shore" to visitors from the east and south.

JOY "Z"

MISCELLANEOUS SLANGUAGE

JC Jersey City

sa CAH cus City of Seacaucus

Da Skyway Pulaski Skyway

Da OYN jez the Oranges: East Orange, West Orange, South Orange, Orange

Bay owner a resident of Bayonne

Big Tuna NY Jets coach Bill Parcells

"You from JAW zee? What exit ya from?" This conversation was made popular during *Saturday Night Live* in the 1980s. If you ask someone from New Jersey this question, they may punch you.

Da Paff Path train from JC to downtown Manhattan
Da Linkin Lincoln Tunnel
Da Haulin' Holland Tunnel

Omaha, Nebraska

Nickname Big O
Most popular phrase "Gobi
    Gred!" (cheer for the
    Cornhuskers heard
    at football games)
Famous local food Runza is
    a sandwich, like a
    Slavic pierogi, from
    the restaurant of the
    same name.

Well-known spot Godfather's. Godfather's Pizza was founded
    in Omaha.
Popular sport/leisure Living and breathing Cornhuskers
    football is a religion here.

MISCELLANEOUS SLANGUAGE

Muddy Mo or Mighty Mo Missouri River
Big Red, Cornhuskers, Huskers, Bugeaters University of
    Nebraska at Lincoln football team
Goin' to Godfather's getting a pizza
The Beef State Nebraska

Penis on the Prairie nickname for our state capitol building
Dodge main road in town
Fred's Big Fred's, a local pizza joint
Mud rocket a fish (bullhead) similar to a catfish
Broncos a very tasty local burger joint

Orange County, California

MISCELLANEOUS SLANGUAGE

Dismal Land Disneyland
"E" ticket ride wild car ride or anything exciting
Passholder anyone with annual pass to Dismal Land who is demanding, rude and snotty
The Big A Anaheim Stadium (last year)
The Big Ed Edison International Field of Anaheim (this year)
Anaslime Anaheim
The Big D Disneyland
No Berry Far Knott's Berry Farm
Hell 91 freeway between Corona and the 55 freeway
San Berdoo San Bernardino

Down the hill high desert reference to going into San Bernardino or LA

PCH Pacific Coast Highway

So Cal Southern California

OC Orange County

Garbage Grove Garden Grove

Behind the Orange Curtain where we are (love it or leave it)

Oriental, North Carolina

MISCELLANEOUS SLANGUAGE

Croaker a fish and an annual festival that makes Oriental famous

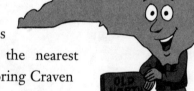

Nurbin New Bern, the nearest city, in neighboring Craven County

RAA pee hoe the town of Arapahoe

Yankee a visiting northerner

Damn Yankee a Yankee who moves here

Collards a leafy vegetable that is second only to grits as a southern delicacy

Pepsi-Cola the local beverage. It was founded in "Nurbin" 100 years ago.

Water shoes white cloth slipperlike shoes for walking on the beach

Orlando, Florida

JAMLANDO

Nicknames O Town, Jam Lando, Orblando, Orland DOH

Most popular phrase You'll often hear "working for the mouse" spoken by those employed by Walt Disney World.

Well-known spot "Die For" is a nickname for the unsafe Highway I-4.

Popular sport/leisure We used to watch the Magic all the time until Shaq left. . . .

MISCELLANEOUS SLANGUAGE

The Parking Lot Interstate 4

Mouse House Walt Disney World

The Trail or OBT Orange Blossom Trail (it's a road)

O-Rena the Orlando Arena (where our Magic play)

A-Coy a nearby small city (Ocoee)

Kiss IH mee nearby town (the accent is on the second syllable)

I-Drive International Drive

Crime Hills Pine Hills (high crime area on the west side)

Least Best Expense Way East West Expressway (toll road)

Penn State

Ya goin' updare State? Do you go to Penn State University?

Joe Pa beloved football coach, aka God! (Some say Saint Joe.)

Stickies favorite pastry served at the diner

The Diner Ye old College Diner

We want sex, we want six heard at all football games

Gray Battleship Beaver Stadium

Foul Mules a sorority

Drugs Unlimited a fraternity

HUB Hetzel Union Building

Mister Sleaze local disco lounge

The Rat the Rathskellar

State Pen Penn State

Philadelphia, Pennsylvania

Nicknames Fill a pa, Fluffya, Philly, Filled Elf Ya, Illadelphia, PhiladelphiYO, Chilladelphia, City of Brotherly Love Handles

Most popular phrase "Yo Adrian" was first heard in *Rocky*. Since then, "yo" has become part of the vernacular everywhere. We'd still like to think that "yo" was made popular by Philadelphians.

Famous local food Cheesesteak Wit. If you like to be humiliated and laughed at, go to Pat's Steaks in South Philadelphia and ask them what the "wit" stands for. Guaranteed they'll line up behind the counter and shout at you "wit fried onions!" Then they'll smile and give you a great sandwich.

YO MUMMER!

Well-known spot Where do all the hippies meet? South Street ("Sail Shtreet").

Popular sport/leisure While not always the most positive bunch, Philadelphians are arguably the most passionate sports fans in the country. Quick to boo and voice their disapproval, they also reward their successful teams with unbridled enthusiasm and cheers.

Most popular song "Fluffya Freedom" by Elton John

MISCELLANEOUS SLANGUAGE

Illadelphia America's rap and hip-hop capital

Sail Shtreet South Street

Sail Fluffya South Philadelphia

Ack a me Acme food store

Fly Guys our beloved hockey team

Dale'n tale'n downtown

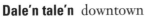

A DAY IN THE LIFE OF A FLUFFYAN

Usually on Sarah Dee or Sunny, we play golf. Out here on the Mikey Tour, we go Don Cobb's Crick, our favorite golf course. Regulars on the tour are D Dawg, Jimbo, Hell Me and THE ALMIGHTY HIGS. Others are Stix Neltone, JP, Eric Pizza, Dutch, Santo Clause, Hercules and Jeff Fraction, the greatest musician the Philadelphia area has ever known (610-695-9585).

The traffic was heavy on the way so we took a few detours. We headed donna Rose Fell Bull Far, thru Conchee, sail'th of King a Presha then donna skuke. Good thing we got annie log brakes.

Nearby Cobb's Crick, we stopped at a WaWa to eat. Yizz always buy a Talian Hoagie, wooder ice, Wishniak and a Goldenbergs. So you might get a little "AH jed ah."

Ail't on the course, we had a baw. I pored a few holes while D-Dawg had two birds and The Almighty Higgs had an iggle. Jimmie Mack had a sandy and an Arnie. Wooder comes into play on a lot of holes and all in all, it was a beauty-full day.

Translation

A DAY IN THE LIFE OF A PHILADELPHIAN

Usually on Saturday or Sunday, we play golf. On the Mikey Tour, we prefer to play down at Cobb's Creek, our favorite golf course. Regulars on the tour, in addition to the Emperor of Slanguage dot com, are D Dawg, Jimbo, Hell Me and THE ALMIGHTY HIGS. Others are Stix Neltone, JP, Eric Pizza, Dutch and Jeff Fraction—the greatest musician the Philadelphia area has ever known.

The traffic was heavy on the way so we took a few

detours. We headed south on the Roosevelt Boulevard, through Conchohocken, south of King of Prussia, then south on the Schuylkill Expressway. Good thing we have anti-lock brakes.

Nearby Cobb's Creek, we stopped at a convenience store, WaWa, to eat. You always buy an Italian sub sandwich, Italian ice, black cherry soda and a peanut chew candy bar. So you might get a little heartburn.

Out on the course, we had a ball. I parred a few holes while Dana had two birdies and Bill had an eagle. Jim parred a hole out of a sand trap and parred another hole without hitting the fairway. Water comes into play on many holes and all in all, it was a beautiful day.

The fail smell made me drop my tail The foul smell made me drop my towel. Often overheard at the pool or donna shore.

Crowns crayons

WaWa convenience store

Mayan or urine mine or yours

Colbert sewer

Ice wooder water with ice

Wooder ice Italian ice or snow

Pie ZAHN Italian friend

Schulkill punch yummy wooder we drink

Sure Kill Distressway exciting road into the city

Iggles

Donna Shore

Yo Adrian

Wooder Ice

Fly Guys

Cheesesteak Wit

Scrapple

PFSF

PHILADELPHIYO!

© 1999 Mike Ellis

SLANGUAGE QUIZ

Manayunk, Conchee, Wissinoming and Passyunk are all

Egg cream is to New York City as Wisniak is to

1) Snowboarders' maneuvers
2) Scottish golf courses
3) Seasonings from Thailand
4) Areas in Philadelphia

1) Salt Lake City
2) Philadelphia
3) Houston
4) Seattle

Wall women, Da Ben, Da Bets some of our bridges

Philly lean correct posture to eat a cheesesteak and keep your clothes clean

Hoagie sub to most

Macaroni and gravy spaghetti and sauce

Tellypole wire place where you throw your old sneakers. You tie your sneakers together so they'll wrap around the wire and stay there, hopefully, for eternity.

School Kill a river and a road

Del Val the extended Fluffya vicinity

The Drives Lincoln and Kelly drives (one on each side of the art museum). They shut down the drives on weekends for blading, biking and walking.

Schlepta public transit

K and A intersection of Kensington and Allegheny avenues

Beg'll wit crim chizz bagel with cream cheese

Egypt, Maui, Baja nighttime hangouts

Ying-Ling popular local beer

Iggles our beloved football team

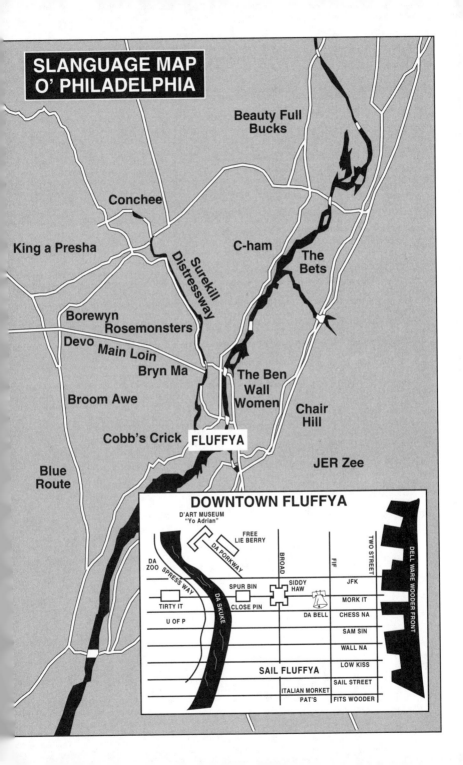

Porked my core parked my car

Phillip the core wid gaz Fill up the car with gasoline.

Li'l Lig your kids play this

Frank or the Big Bambino, Frank Rizzo love him or hate him; the (late) most famous mayor of Philly

Billy Penn the statue of Philadelphia's (and Pennsylvania's) founder, William Penn, which stands high atop City Hall

Mummers groups of (sometimes drunken) men who wear costumes decorated in sequins, glitter and feathers, makeup and sometimes women's clothing, who strut up Broad Street in the freezing cold every New Year's Day. They

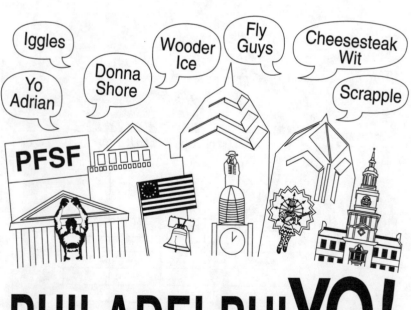

have divisions called the Comics, Fancies, Fancy Brigades and String Bands (who play banjos, accordians, drums, horns and glockenspiels). Sponsored by the city since 1901; started on "Two Street" in South Philly.

Philly Phood Italian wooder ice, soft pretzels (with mustard), scrapple, Tastycakes, Goldenberg's Peanut Chews, cheesesteaks, 'Talian hoagies (on amoroso rolls), Frank's Cherry Wishniak Soda, black and white milkshakes

Philly Suburbs

C-ham Cheltenham
Croydn Beirut
Sham-nee Maw Neshaminy Mall
The Rock Council Rock High School
Delco Delaware county
Rose Monsters girls from a local college
Bryn Ma local college
Borewyn local town
Scroatesville local town
Peckerin' Valley local area
Devo local town and music group
Main Loin wealthy area west of Phila
Beauty-full Bucks beautiful Bucks County suburb
Nervoustown local town

WE ARE DEVO!

Phoenix, Arizona

Most popular phrase An "Arizona cooker" is a car. Anything left inside will melt, warp or die.

Well-known spot When you're going to the BOB, you're taking a trip to watch an Arizona Diamondbacks baseball game here.

Popular sport/leisure Floating down the Salt River is a great way to spend a day tubin' with the locals.

MISCELLANEOUS SLANGUAGE

Fee Nix how we pronounce our city's name

Snots Dale nearby city (glorified suburb)

Tubin' floating down the Salt River

Fone ee shuns us

Tookie Sun city to our south

Sin City retirement community to the west

Dah Fort Fort McDowell Casino, place where snowbirds (especially from Chicago) go

The brown cloud the air in the "valley of the sun"

Smog dogs auto emissions police units

Seizure World retirement community in Mesa

The Deuce seedy downtown district of flophouses and bars (currently being renovated for a big-league baseball stadium)

The Old Pueblo nickname for the city, one of the oldest in Arizona

***A* Mountain** small mountain near the U of Arizona campus, with an *A* painted on it.

Purple Palace America West Arena, where the Suns and Coyotes play

Madhouse on McDowell Veterans Memorial Colliseum (Suns' former home)

BOB Bank One Ballpark, where the AZ Diamondbacks play

PRESS kit how to pronounce Prescott, a city in northern Arizona

The Stack I-10 and I-17 interchange

Short Stack I-10, SR-51 and Loop-202 interchange

Matt a zell the mispronunciation of Mazatzal (a mountain range; also a tribal casino)

Parasite Valley Paradise Valley

NYPD 2 Scottsdale PD (Listen to all the NY accents on a police scanner)

Snobsdale same as Scottsdale/Snotsdale

PV Paradise Valley, pretty much the same as Scottsdale (even right next to it), but even richer and more stuck up

Flag Flagstaff, the summer mountain getaway up north for Phoenicians tired of 110 degree days

Pittsburgh, Pennsylvania

Nicknames Pixburg, D'burg, Urn City, City of Champions

Most popular phrase "Yer such a Yinzer." A derogatory remark among native Pixburgers that makes fun of your local accent. In my opinion, Pittsburgh has one of the most interesting yet unknown accents in the country.

Famous local food Carp and Kolbossa is called Pittsburgh surf and turf.

Well-known spot The Blast Furnace is the place to be when the Steelers are playing and winning.

Popular sport/leisure Western Pennsylvania is a beautiful place where you might find lots of trot (trout) fishermen catching their limits on any given day.

MISCELLANEOUS SLANGUAGE

Sliberty East Liberty

Yinzer Pittsburgher with a strong accent

Kennywood's Open your fly is unzipped

Ought Rought Ett out Route 8

Kernegie Carnegie

Igloo where da Pens play

Pond 16 ounces

I see light local favorite beer

Sputzie sparrow

The Incline tram up Mount Warshington

Gus and Yaya an ices stand on the Nor'side

Car Bill Cowher, coach of the Pixburgh Stillers

Crambry Cranberry, a growing northern suburb

DAWN knee Iris Donnie Iris

The Tubes Liberty Tunnel

Sweeper vacuum cleaner

Picksburgh-ease what we speak

Roller ruler

Grindel tinsel

Ready-o box that polka music comes out of

Korn Bif and Sir Krott corned beef and sauerkraut (a staple in the Pixburger's diet)

Car Par "Cowher power"

Davenport sofa

Rot route—as in, "Turn right onto Rot 51."

Wraught rot

Mon Monongahela River

Yock Youghigheny River

North Fur Sales North Versailles (a small town near Pittsburgh)

The "T" subway/light-rail system

Parts Pittsburgh's baseball team

"Yinz seen a sputzie ettin' a jumbo by the Yock or the MonMon?" Did you see that sparrow eating a balogna sandwich by any of our unpronouncable local rivers?

There are plenty of interesting things to eat and drink in the Burg.

Ham barbecue is thinly chopped ham with ketchup. Heinz is headquartered here.

Some drink soda, some drink pop. Pixburgers drink paw'p.

Lady lox are a local pastry filled with a yummy creamy mousse.

Imp'n Arn is a shot of Imperial and an Iron City beer

Portland, Oregon

Nicknames Stumptown, The Rose City, P Town, Port Town, P.O., Bridgetown, Rip City, Puddletown

Most popular phrase You'll hear "Rip City" when attending a Portland Trailblazers basketball game. It means the fans are happy because the team is scoring.

MISCELLANEOUS SLANGUAGE

Organ our state

Civil War annual football game between the Ducks and the Beavers

Da bridge what Portlanders call the larger bridge to South Portland

Milk Jar Boulevard Martin Luther King Boulevard

The Great Pacific Northwet variation on "Pacific Northwest," due to the amount of rain this area gets

NEP North East Portland

SEP South East Portland

Poh-Hop Portland, Oregon, hip-hop

Silicon Forest high-tech area in outer reaches

Pill Hill OHSU hospital locale

Bridgetown Portland (city has eight bridges that link East to West)

Web Foot native Oregonian

Rose City baby someone born in Portland

The Schnitz Arlene Schnitzer Concert Hall

Trendy-third NW 23rd Avenue, too hip for its own good

Reedie Reed College student

Banfield Interstate 84

Sunset Highway 26

Highway to Hell Route 217, because it's always tied up in both directions

PoPo Portland Police

Hills Burrito Hillsboro, a Portland suburb

Quacker backer University of Oregon Ducks fan

Providence, Rhode Island

Famous local food You have to eat a gagga and a cabinet whenever you visit here. A gagga is our souped-up version of a hot dog, and a cabinet is what most people call a milkshake. People here also like a clam called a quahog.

Gimme a Gagga!

Well-known spot Rizz Dee (RISD—Rhode Island School of Design) is one of the best art schools in the country.

MISCELLANEOUS SLANGUAGE

You Ah Rye University of Rhode Island
Warrick Warwick
Foster-Gloster Foster, Gloucester
Da Creamree Newport Creamery
PawSox Pawtucket Red Sox farm team

Five major food groups in Providence

Quahog A large hard-shell clam. Ask for a "stuffy."
Cab'nit what the rest of the country calls a milkshake
Caw Fee Milkis milk w/coffee-flavored syrup
Soggie a greasy hot dog to the rest of America
Fried Doughboys found at clam stands along Route 1. They're lumps of deep-fried dough.

Marie-er girl's name

Down City downtown Providence

Dels slush-type drink

P't'cket Town of Pawtucket

Yukon University of Connecticut

Leaser's kah Lisa's car

Da hill Federal Hill, Italian part of Providence

Raleigh, North Carolina

Nicknames Rah Lay, Raleigh-wood

Most popular phrase "Hey Bubba" means hello.

Famous local food Lots of fun, interesting things to eat here. Y'all can't miss the pig pickin'. Wash it down with a sweet tea.

Well-known spot CARY is a local town that is rumored to be an acronym for "Containment Area for Relocated Yankees."

Popular sport/leisure Hanging out at D-Bap watching the Durham Bulls is a very enjoyable pastime of the locals.

MISCELLANEOUS SLANGUAGE

Am air goobers those particular peanuts

Tobacco Road where we are

Dean Dome building at a nearby college

Tar heels who we are

Raleighwood Capital of North Carolina, where all the celebs live

Garden peas plain old green peas

Butterbeans young lima beans

Sweet tea iced tea with so much sugar in it that it's essentially uncarbonated Coke. Note that the opposite is not "unsweetened," it's "unsweet."

Pig Pickin' an outdoor festivity in which a pig is cooked over a grill and eaten along with potato salad, coleslaw, hush puppies, and the like

Barbecue not an outdoor gathering, but strictly a type of food made from pig and a vinegar-type sauce. It's what is served at a Pig Pickin'.

The 40 Interstate 40, connecting Raleigh to Durham and Chapel Hill (and the beach)

RTP Research Triangle Park, an area of industrial and office buildings between Raleigh and Durham

D-Bap Durham–Bulls Athletic Park. When I moved to Raleigh I couldn't figure out what they were talking about. Two years later . . . I finally DID figure it out!

Richmond, Virginia

Well-known spot Excellent nightlife can be found at the Bottom.

Popular sport/leisure We enjoy shopping at the Slip.

MISCELLANEOUS SLANGUAGE

Duh Rivah James River

The Vapors how ladies respond to the subtropical climate in central Virginia

Warsh 'em stanky dawgs Wash your smelly feet.

FFV's First Families of Virginia

You Krops where FFV's buy their groceries

Lee, Jackson, King Day January holiday celebrated in Richmond

The Slip Shockoe Slip, popular shopping district

The Bottom Shockoe Bottom (good nightlife)

West End geographic location between Richmond and Charlottesville

Po' White not white trash, but a local expressway: Powhite (from Powhatan Indians)

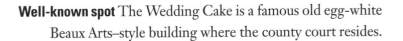

Riverside, California

Well-known spot The Wedding Cake is a famous old egg-white Beaux Arts–style building where the county court resides.

MISCELLANEOUS SLANGUAGE

Berdoo San Bernardino, the competitive cousin of Riverside

Mo Vall Moreno Valley, nearby bedroom community

Crowntown Corona, an Orange County wanna-be community to the west

Mag Magnolia Avenue, our sometimes toney main street through town

Rollover Clover our primary, dangerous, thrill-ride freeway interchange of the 91–60–215 routes

Cresties rich people who live in "Canyon Crest"

O Rs (pronounced "oh-are's") for Old Riversiders, empty nesters and retirees who always seem to get low interest rates, invited to Mayor's breakfasts, etc.

91 main freeway spine through town

Lake Al blues and jazz joint known also as "Lake Alice," in center of downtown

Vicky's Orange Victoria's Orange, a popular eatery downtown

Eye E short for Inland Empire

Oh See short for Orange County

Roob a Doo lame way to say Rubidoux (part of Riverside)

Nor Cow lame way of saying Norco, a suburb of Riverside

Home Garbage lame way of saying Home Gardens, part of Corona

The Platter Mad Platter, the record store in Riverside

Rochester, New York

Nicknames Rah Cha Cha, Rottenchester

Most popular phrase "Like lilacs and white hots." This refers to eating our famous white hot dogs at our May lilac festival.

Famous local food The Garbage Plate is a menu item from Nick Tahou Hots. You get either hot dogs or hamburgers with home fries, macaroni, salad, lots and lots of onions, mustard and hot sauce all slopped together on one plate.

Well-known spot The Nipple of Knowledge is the top of the main library at the University of Rochester (the architecture is a bit phallic, to say the least).

MISCELLANEOUS SLANGUAGE

Chye Lye Chili, a suburb

ER the suburb of East Rochester, not a television show

Sha LOTT Charlotte, the neighborhood where the beach is found

U of R the University of Rochester

The South Wedge the triangular-shaped neighborhood south of downtown

Demagogue and Comical *The Democrat & Chronicle* (D&C), local newspaper

X rocks　Xerox, where you work if you don't work at Kodak

I RUN da quit　Rochester bay suburb otherwise known as Irondequiot

Greece　a suburb, not a country

Kodak　God, with 30,000 employees in the city

Flour/Flower City　town nickname

The Strip　Lake Avenue

White hot　a thick-skinned white hot dog invented in Rochester. A little spicier than your normal dog.

Sacramento, California

Nicknames　Sack o' Tomatoes, Sack Toe, Sack Town, Sacred Men's Toes

Most popular phrase　"What's in Sack?" You might hear this when somebody's trying to find something to do in Sacramento.

Well-known spot　The Darth Vader is a building downtown which has a dour resemblance to the movie character

MISCELLANEOUS SLANGUAGE

K Street　downtown mall

Old Sack　Old Sacramento

The Valley　reference to San Joaquin Valley

The Fab 40s between J Street and Folsom Boulevard from 40th to 49th streets

I-80 called the Capital City Freeway or Biz 80

The W-X section of Capital City Freeway between I-5 and Highway 99, which is between (parallel to) W Street and X Street

Sac State California State University, Sacramento

Saint Louis, Missouri

Nickname Sane LUE We

Most popular phrase "I pray to the lard." This mispronunciation is heard every Sunday at churches throughout St. Louis. There is no can of Crisco anywhere to be found.

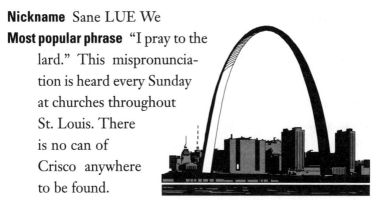

Famous local food All locals go to the Hill for fine Italian food.

Well-known spot If somebody in St. Louis goes to MIT, they just might be attending Merrimac in Town (Merrimac Community College).

Popular sport/leisure Mark McGwire of the St. Louis Cardinals is worshiped both here and abroad for his baseball prowess.

MISCELLANEOUS SLANGUAGE

Farty Far major roadway

Fo Po Forest Park

I go to Warsh U I go to Washington University

Slew Saint Louis University

Sauget Ballet (pronounced Saw Jet) Eastside topless dance club area

LA Lower Arnold, suburb just outside of St. Louis

Innerbelt I-170, highway through St. Louis

Fo Po Cocoa Forest Park Community College

Ted Drewes St. Louis's renowned frozen custard stand

The White Rat Whitey Herzog

Dogtown a Southside neighborhood with cool bars

The Tiv Tivoli theater

Charlie Town St. Charles

Shart opposite of tall

Traffic cart where you go when you've been caught speeding

Mo Bap Missouri Baptist College

PSB Poplar Street bridge

Snoots fried pigs' noses

UCLA Upper Corner of Lower Arnold

Big Mac Mark McGwire

The Wizard Ozzie Smith

T-ravs toasted ravioli, a totally St. Louis thing

When you're visiting St. Louis and you feel like stopping by the zoo in the middle of the night to wake all the animals, make like the teenagers and yell, "Funark, funark, funark."

MO BO RO Missouri Bottom Road

Silly Hall St. Louis City Hall

The Blanchette the I-70 dual bridges—four lanes each way, crossing over the Missouri River connecting NW St. Louis County to St. Charles County

Car Vett a classic car we drive

Salt Lake City, Utah

Nicknames SLC, Behind the Zion Curtain

Most popular phrase "Oh my golly heck" is the most severe curse you'll ever hear uttered here.

BREED 'EM YOUNG UNIVERSITY

Famous local food Virgin Marys are a popular beverage.

Well-known spot Brigham Young University is a famous

Some Mormon abbreviations or acronyms

MO Mormon

Mo Town Provo

Mo Gul large white bird

Mo Peds downtown walkers

Mo Lasses Mormon babes

Mo Sey Mormon sense of time

Mo Tif Mormon fight

Mo Mo's Mormons

Mormon college located here. Rumor has it that BYU really stands for Breed 'em Young University, due to their having one of the highest birth rates of any college campus.

Popular sport/leisure On the Brigham Young campus, you might hear people refer to "NCMO" (pronounced "nick-mo"). It stands for Noncommital Makeout. Even though it's something of a sin in the Mormon community, it's an epidemic anyway.

MISCELLANEOUS SLANGUAGE

The "Y" Brigham Young University (not YMCA)

Gentile a non-Mormon

Fetch Mormon for the "F" word

Zoobie BYU student

Jack-Mormon the same as a lapsed Catholic or a backsliding Baptist

Urine Utah You are in Utah.

Slic Salt Lake Community College

The Salt Salt Lake City

Leggo Cruz da State Let's go cruise State Street.

SLOC (pronounced Slock) Salt Lake Olympic Committee

Bribery what happened to SLOC

BMW Big Mormon Wagon

MST Mormon Standard Time, instead of Mountain Standard Time

LMAV Large Mormon Attack Vehicles

American Fark American Fork

Spanish Fark Spanish Fork

San Antonio, Texas

Nicknames San TONY Oh, San ANN Tone, San Tone, San Tone

Most popular phrase "Anybody knows beans 'bout chili knows chili ain't got no beans!"

Famous local food When you order meat in a restaurant, you might say, "Knock the horns off, wipe its ass and drag it in," if you want your steak rare. Don't forget that armadillo eggs are really stuffed Jalepeño peppers.

Well-known spot The Alamo is a symbol of pride to all Texans. Also a place where Ozzy Osbourne took a pee pee popper.

Popular sport/leisure We love Da Spurs, the 1999 NBA Champs!

MISCELLANEOUS SLANGUAGE

Hill Country Central Texas
Chick'n fried steak battered and fried beef cut—state food
UTSA University of Texas at San Antonio

Riverwalk stretch of the San Antonio River that winds through scenic parts of the city

Hippie Hollow swimming hole near Austin, where hippies and the like can frequently be found skinny-dipping and doing drugs

Armadillah state hood ornament

Holler if ya need anythang! Kindly state your needs at the appropriate time!

09 used to refer to a resident of Alamo Heights, a pricey suburb of San Antonio

San Diego, California

Nicknames Los Sandiegoles, Sandy Eggo

Famous local food I'm going to get a cab. This is a Carne Asada Burrito.

Well-known spot Many visitors take a peek at Black's Beach. It's the largest nude beach in the country.

Popular sport/leisure A reference to a coyote may mean someone who helps illegal aliens cross the border from Mexico.

MISCELLANEOUS SLANGUAGE

PB the community of Pacific Beach

OB the community of Ocean Beach

Los Angelesization to make like Los Angeles

The Stand Silver Stand State Park and beach

The Cove La Jolla Cove, in the affluent part of SD

TJ Tijuana, Mexico

The Coaster a commuter train that runs between Oceanside and downtown San Diego

Del Martian person from Del Mar (a suburb of San Diego)

Banzai Runner illegal alien who sprints through the checkpoint into the U.S., hoping not to get caught

The Del short for Hotel del Coronado, a very fashionable resort

The 'Dres (The Drays) short for the Padres baseball team

Over-the-Line a baseball-like tournament played each summer on Fiesta Island

The Murph Jack Murphy Stadium

The Merge traffic nightmare where I-5 and I-805 join

The Pods our baseball team

The Qualisium what San Diegan's call Qualcomm Stadium

The 'Bah the Casbah, very popular alternative nightclub and venue in downtown San Diego

The WAP the San Diego Zoo Wild Animal Park, as it is lovingly called by the locals

BS Borrego Springs

Whompers a beach in La Jolla with BIG waves

San Francisco, California

Nicknames San Fran Disco, Saint Freak-show, Frisco, San Fantastico, Bagdad by the Bay

Most popular phrases Locals often refer to their BMW when they don't even own a car. BMW here means Bart, Muni and Walkin', the three main modes of transportation in the city. Someone who is "Gilman Street" is someone who is very punk—924 Gilman Street is found in Berkeley.

Famous local food You have to try a Joe's Special. A mixture of ground beef and spinach scrambled in eggs. There are now three Joe's Restaurants.

Well-known spot The Castro is a famous gay neighborhood here.

Popular sport/leisure We live and die with the 49ers. We become Forty Whiners when they lose.

MISCELLANEOUS SLANGUAGE

The Lake Lake Tahoe
Berzerk Lee Berkeley
Multimedia Gulch area south of Market, rejuvenated by multimedia companies
3COM the Stick

Barted into the city and ferried back took the train into San Fran and the boat to get back

South City South San Francisco

Out East Sacramento

The Rock Alcatraz

The Gate Golden Gate Bridge

Red and White ferries that run to Vallejo

The wine country Mission Street between 5th and 8th, hangout for winos

The Mish Mission District

Nickel-dime refers to the East Bay's 510 area code

The Peninsula any town south of South City up to San Jose (as long as it's on the west side [ocean side] of the bay)

Hay weird East Bay town of Hayward

Freakmont East Bay town of Fremont

Fagdad by the Bay an improvement on "Bagdad by the Bay"

Coco County Contra Costa County (across the bay from SF)

The Swish Alps hilly area above Castro Street (the gay neighborhood)

The City of Brotherly Love gay SF

The Maze place on 580 and 680 where the highways intersect

Advertising Gulch Area by the Embarcadero from Pacific Avenue to Levi's Plaza

Snob Hill Nob Hill

The F the F Market streetcar line (God bless it)

The Glass Coffin the Twin Peaks bar

The Mark the Mark Hopkins Hotel

The Washbag the Washington Square Bar & Grill

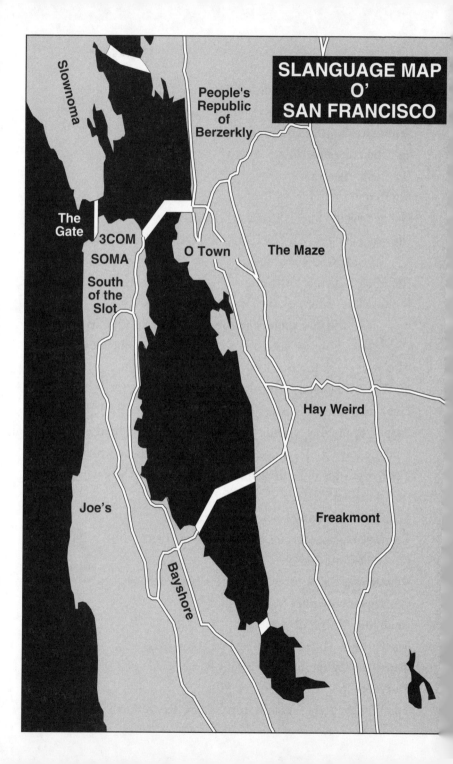

Divizz Divisadero Street

The Maytag St. Mary's Cathedral (looks like a washing machine agitator, but is intended to have a roof and walls shaped with a holy cross facing heaven)

The Bayshore Highway 101

Nasty Nimitz 880 on East Bay

PRB as in, "Please excuse his/her attitude . . . he/she lives in the PRB" (People's Republic of Berkeley).

The avenues as in, "I live in the avenues now" (Richmond/Sunset districts of SF).

Going to the snow going skiing in the Sierra Nevada mountains

The Dunce Cap the TransAmerica Building

R, B or G? Richmond Bridge, Bay Bridge, or Golden Gate Bridge?

Chocolate Square Ghirardelli Square

Fortune cookie row Chinatown

Sushi row Japan town

Hairy Tongues Harrington's, an Irish yuppie bar in the Financial District

Oak Town Oakland

Slow no ma Sonoma County

Rodent Parts City of Rohnert Park, in Sonoma County

His Willieness San Francisco's most Honorable Mayor Willie Brown

SOMA more correct spelling of South of Market

The TL Tenderloin District

South of the Slot South of Market Street (the slot was for the street car cable)

WPOD White Punks on Dope, young people of the Sunset District

---

San Jose, California

Nickname San Hoe

Most popular phrase
"Are we all Santa Bar-barians?"

JOSÉ CAN YOU SEE

Well-known spot Locals might confuse you when they mention Bedwetter's Beach for Ledbetter's Beach.

Popular sport/leisure Hanging out at the Shark Tank watching our beloved hockey team is a favorite pastime.

Most popular song "Do You Know the Way to San Jose?"

MISCELLANEOUS SLANGUAGE

The South Bay where we live

The Arena where the Sharks play

Hayweird nearby town of Hayward

Coop nearby city of Cupertino

Hellway Guadalupe Parkway during rush hour

The Pass Highway 154 (San Marcos Pass Road)

IV Isla Vista (the college town)

Santa Barbarians or Santa Babalonians what we call ourselves

Ro Co Santa Barbara Roasting Company (a local coffee house)

The Snooze Press our fishwrap, *The News-Press*

Brookie Brooks Photography Institute student

Masonite one who lives on the Mesa

Useless Beast University of California Santa Barbara (UCSB), also known as "You Can Study Buzzed"

Cito Rats kids from the wealthy suburb of Montecito

Scranton, Pennsylvania

Most popular phrase "It's a nice day, hayna?"

Famous local food Two things you might find here are whimpies, which are what most call Sloppy Joes. Peer OH gees are a local treat which are supposed to be potatoes.

Well-known spot Everybody here shops at De Eynon, the old Sugarman's shopping center.

MISCELLANEOUS SLANGUAGE

Hayna? Isn't it true?

Da U University of Scranton

Down da line shopping route for Northeast Pennsylvania

Cuppa, too, tree a few things

Outta fill 'em, Haynah? Out of camera film, aren't you?
Plimmit Plymouth, Pennsylvania
Turdy-ate WOLF-TV, Channel 38
Nanny Coke across the river from West Nanny Coke
Tarupe Troop, Pennsylvania
ACK a mee the place where you get da grocery order
Down Steamtown the other mall across town

Seattle, Washington

Nicknames Latteland, Emerald
    City, Seatown
Most popular phrase "Watch out for
    the Seattle BO." After three
    days of no rain, the smog
    takes over and the city needs
    a shower to cleanse itself. You
    also might hear "It rains here
    all the time." It's actually a
    catch phrase to limit popula-
    tion growth.
Famous local food "Gimme a
    skinny six-shooter on
    the mountain." This will get you a six-shot latte on ice
    with non-fat milk.
Well-known spot For a beautiful view, visit the Space Noodle.
Popular sport/leisure Mike Holmgren's got our football team
    cooking these days.

MISCELLANEOUS SLANGUAGE

Slug Seattle's official animal

Moss Seattle's official plant

Seattlites our own nickname

Harborzoo Harborview hospital

World's largest Chia Pet the Kingdome, with moss growing
on top

SoDo south of the Kingdome

SMHI Seattle Museum of Hysteria & Indecision (Seattle
Mental Health Institute)

Space Noodle Space Needle (tourist attraction)

Tuk Chuck Tukwila Police

Hellvue Bellevue

Deadmond Edmonds or Redmond (true in both cases)

Moneydina Medina (home of Bill Gates)

Snohickish Snohomish

Pukeallup Puyallup

Learn how to order coffee. This ain't New York, where you
only have to say "coffee, regular." Here's a quick primer to
help you talk like the world's experts on ordering coffee in
Seattle:

Double Moe, Skinny with Sticks and a Punch I'd like a double
mocha with non-fat milk, straws and my punch card
marked.

Why Bother I'd like a decaf latte with non-fat milk.

Skinny Six-shooter on the Mountain I'd like a six-shot latte with
non-fat milk on ice.

Stinkoma Tacoma (it does smell, as does Smellingham [Bellingham])

Jerkland Kirkland

Traffic-light-wood Lynnwood

Neverit Everett

Catholic Hill area of many churches

The Pencil building Rainier Tower, a downtown skyscraper that is narrower at its base than the rest of the tower

Grab the Princess ride the *Princess Marguerite III* to Victoria, British Columbia

Blahvue boring corporate suburb of Bellevue

Weedle on the Needle blinking red light on the top of the Space Needle

South Jersey

Nicknames Donna Shore, Dale'n'Jerz, Sail'th Jersey

Most popular phrase "Did you see those chicks from Quee Beak? Damn."

Famous local food Jersey tomatoes are awaited all year by many people.

Well-known spots There are many beautiful towns here on the ocean, such as Sleaze Side, Senile City and Stoned Harbor.

Popular sport/leisure The locals like to complain about the visitors who flood the shore every weekend and throughout the summer. They might call them Shoebies or WEBs. Shoebies were tourists who visited the shore many years ago and carried their possessions in shoeboxes. WEB is an acronym for Week End Bastards.

MISCELLANEOUS SLANGUAGE

Bennies tourists from North Jersey with black socks

Pie Knee South Jersey native

Sakakas Seacacus, New Jersey

Mars Town Morristown, New Jersey

The Shore anything south of the Raritan river

Norker someone from Newark

Green Crick Green Creek, New Jersey

Freehole Freehold, New Jersey

Mommith County Monmouth County

Bwuh bwah telephone conversation ending

Marburr brand of cigarettes

Sleaze Side Seaside, popular seaside spot in South Jersey

Churry Hill town over the river from Phila

Deafer Depford, New Jersey

Sailth Jersey that's us

Dell Member short for Delaware Memorial Bridge

AC Atlantic City

EHT Egg Harbor Township

Fingerboard a junction of three or more roads at one point

Traffic circle another Jersey highway oddity

Clam diggers natives of coastal towns in Ocean County, such as Manahawkin, Tuckerton, etc.

Senile City Sea Isle City

Stoned Harbor Stone Harbor

Spokane, Washington

Nicknames Spokanowhere, Spookaloo, Lilac City

Most popular phrase Spokane is the "spoon-size town with the spoon-size name."

Famous local food Visit Heartburn Road when you're here. Division Street is called this because of the traffic problems and the concentration of restaurants.

Well-known spot Go to Dick's Run for a good hamburger.

Popular sport/leisure The Bloomsday Race is an internationally known, 7.5-mile race that takes place here every year. Fifty thousand "Bloomies" participate in this foot race, which is usually won by a skinny Kenyan.

Easiest way to get someone from Spokane mad at you Ask them, "Aren't you a suburb of Seattle?"

MISCELLANEOUS SLANGUAGE

Wet side/Wetsider someone from the Western Washington/ Seattle area

CDA the city of Couer D'Alene, Idaho, our nearby neighbor
Snob Hill South Hill area of Spokane
NYE knee Interstate 90
395 also known as Division Street

Springfield, Illinois

Nickname Springpatch
Most popular phrase "Here come the Grovers."
   A reference to the strict Leland Grove
   police force.
Famous local food The Horseshoe is a piece
   of toast covered with French fries and
   cheese sauce.
Well-known spot The War Zone is the area
   where Cubs and Cardinals fans overlap.
Popular sport/leisure We might hang out at
   Lake Lepto. You have to be careful of the
   microscopic critters found living in Lake
   Springfield.

MISCELLANEOUS SLANGUAGE

You iz University of Illinois at Springfield (UIS)
Sag a Mon Sangamon County
The Grove & J'rome our two unincorporated towns within the
   town
The Carillon world's tallest belltower

Tampa Bay, Florida

MISCELLANEOUS SLANGUAGE

The Bucs our football team
The Big Sombrero where the Bucs play
Malfunction Junction I-4 and I-275
    loop
The Frankenstein The Howard Frank-
    land Bridge
E-bor Ybor City, happening section of Tampa
Done eatin' Dunedin, small city west of Tampa
Da Bolts Tampa Bay Lightning, NHL team
Cigar City another name for Tampa, Florida

Tucson, Arizona

Nicknames Prune Valley, Medicare Acres,
    Geritol Junction

MISCELLANEOUS SLANGUAGE

Green Valley a retirement community
    just south of Tucson
Scum Tran our bus system (Sun Tran)
Amphibians students at Amphitheater
    High School

Crappola de Tucson term for "Corona de Tucson" (a sort of suburb)

CRAP water name for the disastrous CAP (Central Arizona Project) water fiasco

Suicide lane center lane on major streets that is thru traffic in one direction during some hours, thru traffic in another direction during other hours, and left-turn-only all other hours

The Lemon Mt. Lemon

Washington, DC

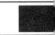

Nickname District of Crack

Most popular phrase You'll often hear people discussing Beltway Bandits. They are outfits that do a lot of business with the government. The name implies a lot of things, especially SCAM.

Famous local food Bean pies are sold by local vendors.

Well-known spots There are a lot of touristy spots to visit, such as the Mall, the Hill and the Gourmet. Also, the Metro is an excellent subway system.

Popular sport/leisure The Pressure Cooker, Jack Kemp Cooke Stadium, is the new home of the Skins.

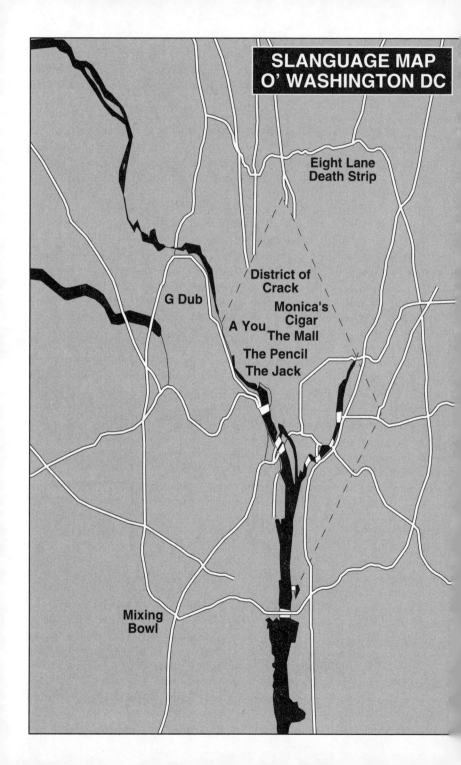

MISCELLANEOUS SLANGUAGE

The Hill where laws are made, where bars are visited

Downtown what people call the city

The Mall where the monuments are, where the tourists are

DC what people call the city (District of Crack, after the infamous episode involving the mayor)

The Skins the Washington Redskins football team

The Birds the Orioles baseball team

The Jack where the Skins play, also features large rock concerts

The Gourmet as in the Gourmet Giant (Giant grocery stores), where the pretentious go to buy groceries—located in the posh suburbs

Blank stare Washington greeting

The Metro public transportation

Beltway Bandit consulting company that does lots of government business

Inside the Beltway the more desirable place to live

Ellipse park behind White House; nothing to do with the moon

FOB Friend of Bill's

Mixing bowl the I-395, I-495 (Beltway) and I-95 intersection

Eight-lane Deathstrip 495 Beltway that circles the city

The Pencil Washington monument

Slick Willys a nightclub at Capitol Hill

Chelsey's a nightclub in Georgetown, DC

The Phone Booth the MCI Center

Wilmington, Delaware

Nickname Womanton

Most popular phrase Slower Delaware, we
  are NOT.

Famous local food Arsters are a popular bottom feeder.

Well-known spot The Arster Eat is the number two social event of the year.

Popular sport/leisure Don't miss the Punkin' Chuckin' event.
  A Sussex County event where pumpkins are thrown for
  distance. The record is nearly a mile.

MISCELLANEOUS SLANGUAGE

New Ark Please don't call it "Noork."

Diversity of Underwear Newark's most hallowed institution

The Bob Bob Carpenter Center at the Diversity of Underwear

I sawl it I viewed it with my own eyes.

Louis how to say "Lewes"

EVery AMEriCan CiTy's SLANGuage

I thought all these phrases began in Philadelphia. It was the first place I heard them and I wrongly assumed their origin was in my hometown of Philadelphia.

These phrases were submitted by thousands of people from hundreds of cities who also assumed that these phrases originated in their hometown.

The bottom line: These phrases are spoken by millions of people in thousands of cities.

Jeet? No, Joo? "Did you eat?" "No, did you?"

Flars flowers

Pars powers

Shars showers

Sar sour

Tar tower

Kwar choir

Dar dire

Far fire

Har higher

Lar liar

Plars pliers

Tars tires

Wars wires

Fit hit the shan shit hit the fan

Dootcher as in Dootcher Momma tells ya

Hasta la pasta! See ya later.

Been that . . . done there rather than usual reverse

Usetacould I could do it then, but I am not able to do it now.

Birds are flying Your bra straps are showing.

Aorta . . . They ought to . . .

Al owl

Crick creek

ruf roof

Usage example I sawn al, on the ruf a the shack down by th'
    crick.

DINKWAD Double Income No Kids With A Dog (a couple
    with no kids and a dog)

Prairie Doggin' to pop up from your cubicle at work to see
    what is going on, who came back from lunch, what that
    noise was, etc.

That dog'll hunt That should work.

That dog won't hunt That will not work.

ADIDAS All Day I Dream About Sex

Zinc where you wash your dishes

Warsh wash

Warshington Washington

Over yonder directions for that-a-way

Youse plural form of "you." Syntactically identical to "Y'all"
    or "You all."

Dis, Dat, Deez, Doze this, that, these, those

How ya doan? Yite? How are you doing? Are you all right?

Yoots youths

Burl boil

Earl oil

Lemme lookinsee Let me investigate.

Sittin' on da stoop sitting on the front or back steps

Da bum a less than stellar sports player

Kegger party with beer kegs

FOReign SLANGuages

If you can speak English, you can speak a foreign language. There are over 500,000 words in English and they all mean something in another language. You can speak a foreign language because you already know the words.

Till now, all methods for teaching a language have been a scam. Slanguage can teach anyone a language without wasting time the old way.

Draw your own pictures to help with memorizing. Someday soon, everybody will effortlessly speak dozens of languages. Watch for the moronic devices at the bottom of all the pages of foreign cities.

Here's a bunch of English words that mean something else in another language.

Key? French for "Who?" (*Qui?*) or Spanish (*Qui?*). *Key* also refers to an inner strength everyone has in Japanese.

Ohio Japanese for "good morning"

Bong Korean for "bread"

Gift German for "poison" (*gift*)

Do We Ski? French for "Some whiskey?" (*Du whiskey?*)

Cone GOOSE Toe Spanish for "with pleasure" (*con gusto*)

Cone Spanish for "with" (*con*)

Belly Italian for "handsome" (*belli*)

Guy Jean Japanese for "foreigner"

Ho Cantonese for "fine"

Bow French for "nice" or "handsome" (*beau*)

Bell French for "beautiful" (*belle*)

English Words I Betcha Didn't Know Were Foreign Curses

Warning: These are fighting words in their respective countries.

Peace French for "peepee" (*pisse*)

Shot French for "women's private spot" (*chatte*)

Beet French for "men's private part" (*bite*)

Cooly Italian for "butthole" (*culi*)

She-eh French for "pooping" (*chier*)

Bet French for "idiot" (*bête*)

Pet French for "cut the cheese" (*péte*)

Cool or Cooly (like Grand Coulee Dam) or **Coolio** (like the rap/hip hop artist) all mean butthole in many cities, such as Madrid, Rome and Mexico City.

Moronic Devices
Use these images to help you speak a foreign language.
For example, "Pong Yo" is Mandarin Chinese for "friend."
"Cone GOOSE Toe" is Spanish for "with pleasure."

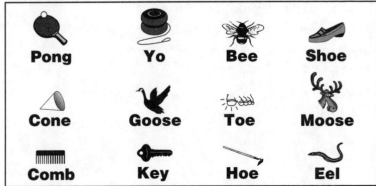

Saying something as simple as "Cool" in Madrid or Rome may get a few of the locals upset with you. On the other hand, the locals will crack up if you use these words as a friend, having fun with them. They also might be more than a little impressed that you can talk just like the locals.

Let's string together a few to really wake 'em up. Be forewarned: Many of these words are quite powerful and may make people mad. Remember that you are outnumbered in a foreign country with few laws in your favor.

2A-Bet French for "You're a fool" (*Tu es bête*)

Say Doo PeePee Don French for "That's donkey peepee" (*C'est dupipi d'âne*)

Key Pet? French for "Who's cutting the cheese?" (*Qui pète?*)

FOREIGN SLANGUAGE QUIZ

Match the left SLANGUAGE phrase with the correct translation on the right.

May GOOSE Tah	Chinese for "Hello."
Tee Connies?	French for "To the pool."
Eel Fay BOW	Spanish for "I like it."
Joe Say "K"	French for "Some Whiskey?"
Chow Bellow	Greek for "How are you?"
Knee How Ma?	French for "It's a nice day."
Allah Pea SCENE	Spanish for "I know what?"
Do We SKI?	Italian for "Hi, handsome."

Aberdeen, Scotland

Div ya hay a fag? Do you have a cigarette?

Chapit taties mashed potatoes

Are ya cummin ta see mi the morns morn?
   Are you visiting tomorrow?

Lassie girl

Bam fool

Fit foot

Hoose house

Aye, aye, fit like the day? Hello, how are you today?

Hud yer wheesht! Shut up!

Eye yes

War ya gone? Where are you going?

Pure dead brilliant so it is an that good (appreciation of something)

Sleek it small

Hogmanay New Year's Eve

Hoolet owl

Maw mother

Poo pull

Skite slip

Sook suck

Tap top

Wrang wrong

Albany, Western Australia

Boof head dummy
Bonza very good
Strike me pink I am very surprised.
Peanut idiot
Monarch aboriginal slang for police
      officer
Ridgy didge legitimate item or
      comment
Punchy prone to fight at the drop of a hat (lit-
      tle provocation)
Stubbie glass bottle containing beer (Emu Export, Fosters)
Whinger someone prone to constantly vocalizing discontent

Athens, Greece

If you can speak English, you can speak Fun Greek Slanguage. Without even trying, you'll be talking
like the locals. You can speak Fun Slanguage because you already know the
words. I've rearranged them to
come out in another language.

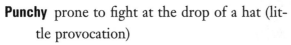

   Read the large, English
phrase with emphasis on the ALL
CAPS syllable or word. Say the phrase
quickly yet smoothly. Believe it or not,

you're speaking another language. The translations follow. At the bottom of page 142, you'll find pictures that I call moronic devices. Use these pictures to help you pronounce and memorize phrases.

We should have been learning it this way all along. Slanguage is the beginning of the end of language barriers.

Tee Connnies? How are you?
Pole LEEK'll La Very well.
FEE lay friend
SUE pa soup
Elly YES olives
Coat TOE pool oh chicken
Doe MA tess tomatoes
Pa POO Grandpa
YA ya Grandma
POP see Be quiet.
Tee? What?
Neigh yes
OH he no
Boo ZOO key jamming Greek music and dance

Let's string together a few phrases to really sound impressive.

Tee connie fee lay? Poe LEEK'll la How are you, friend? Very well.

This section of Greek Slanguage dedicated to Arthur, Sophia, Christo and Michael Gougolis of Brooklawn, New Jersey.

Auckland, New Zealand

Nickname We accept the fact that people call us Kiwis.

Most popular phrase *Bloody oath* means "That's great."

Famous local food Shark and taties is known elsewhere as fish and chips.

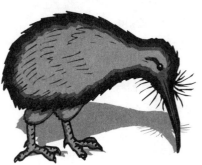

MISCELLANEOUS SLANGUAGE

Cher bro That's good, yes.

Mmm-no pretending to think about saying no when you already have made your mind up

Pakeha European person (white man)

He's a bit of a dog he has a good sense of humor

Get stuffed be quiet

Ah, yeah gidday, mate. How's it Garn? Hi.

Bach vacation home/cottage

Cockie farmer

Cow cockie cow (esp. dairy) farmer

kiwi New Zealander (or a small flightless bird, definitely not a green-fleshed fruit)

The mainland South Island

Prang crash

West Island Australia

> **Rattle your dags** Hurry up
> Dags are the bits of dried poop that hang off the wool of
> sheep. They rattle when they move.

Tea dinner
Sparky electrician
Ridgie didge that will be fine
Jendles sandals, thongs, open shoes
Hokey Pokey a flavor of ice cream (sort of honeycomb)
Gone for a tiki (tickey) tour to take oneself off on a self-guided
  tour of unfamiliar surroundings

Barcelona, Spain

If you can speak English, you can speak
Spanish Slanguage. Without even trying, you'll be talking like the locals.
You can speak Fun Slanguage
because you already know the words.
I've rearranged them to come out in
another language.

Read the large, English phrase with
emphasis on the ALL CAPS word. Say
the phrase quickly yet smoothly.
Believe it or not, you're speaking

another language. The translations follow. At the bottom of page 142, you'll find pictures that I call moronic devices. Use these pictures to help you pronounce and memorize phrases.

We should have been learning it this way all along. Slanguage is the beginning of the end of language barriers.

Boo WAYNE as SNOW chase Good evening (*Buenas noches*)
Kay DEE say? What do you say? (*Que dice?*)
No MOOCH oh, two? Not much, yourself? (*No mucho, tú?*)
Cone DEE owes With God (*Con Dios*)
COMB oh VAH? How's it going? (*Como va?*)
Bee YEN ee two? Fine, and yourself? (*Bien y tú?*)
Bee YEN Fine (*Bien*)
DONE day? Where? (*Donde?*)
Low see YEN toe I'm sorry (*Lo siento*)
Moment TEE toe In a moment (*momentito*)
See two low DEE says If you say so (*Si tú lo dices*)

Beijing, China

If you can speak English, you can speak Mandarin Slanguage. Without even trying, you'll be talking like the locals. You can speak Fun Slanguage because you already know the words. I've rearranged them to come out in another language. Fun Chinese Slanguage isn't the hardest language in the world. It's the easiest.

Read the large, English phrase with emphasis on the ALL CAPS word. Say the phrase quickly yet smoothly. Believe it or not, you're speaking another language. The translations follow. At the bottom of page 142, you'll find pictures that I call moronic devices. Use these pictures to help you pronounce and memorize phrases.

We should have been learning it this way all along. Slanguage is the beginning of the end of language barriers.

Knee how hello
Knee how ma? How are you?
How fine
How how how very very well
Shay shay thank you
Hen how very good
Pong yo friend
Dim sum literally "touch the heart," little appetizers
Fong pay I must have eaten beans.
May yo I don't have it.
Eye knee love you
Pee Joe beer
Ma horse, mother or scold (meaning depends on intonation)
Cha tea
Hoy lake

Let's string together a few phrases:

Knee how ma pong yo? How how how, shay shay "How are you, friend?" "Fine fine fine, thank you."

This section dedicated to Tom, Joannie, Taylor and Lexi King.

Belfast, Northern Ireland

Owzaboutye How are you?
Norn Iron where Belfast is
Gimma head peace! Be quiet, or Quit your
  teasing.
Bout'ye, howsit goin', gettin' it handy?
  How are you, keeping well?
Your bum's out the winda You're talking
  rubbish.
You're talking through your hat same as
  above
Half the lies you tell aren't true I don't know whether to
  believe you or not.

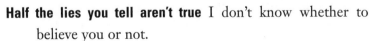

The crack was 90 It was an excellent time. (Crack [spelled criac] has nothing to do with drugs in Ireland.)

Brisbane, Australia

Briz Bin how to correctly pronounce Brisbane

Dugger idiot or loser

Turn it up get serious

Crook ill

The guy is a tool The guy is a real loser!

Togs swimsuit

Cheerios small, red sausages . . . also called little boys

Joey infant kangaroo

The 'gabba the Woolloongabba sporting arena . . . cricket often played here

Yank tank large American car

Vegemite salty spread on toast and bread (takes an acquired taste)

Brisbane is pronounced BRIZ Bin. Pronounce it any other way and you're branded a tourist.

Calgary, Alberta, Canada

Nickname Some call us Cow Town.

Most popular phrase Americans are a bunch of useless, gun-toting fools.

Famous local food We enjoy a session of imbibing wobbly pop, known elsewhere as alcohol.

Well-known spot The Stampede is the world-famous Calgary Exhibition and Stampede Rodeo.

Popular sport/leisure We love to spend a day stampeding at the Stampede.

MISCELLANEOUS SLANGUAGE

Red Square Petro-Canada Corporate Headquarters (Calgary landmark)

Iceberg Calgary City Hall

Princess Island Prince's Island Park, popular downtown park

Lert local light-rail rapid transit train (also called C-Train)

Plus 15 elevated, covered pedstrian bridges over streets

Saddledome local NHL hockey arena

Trails mini-freeways within the city

Junior small oil company

Freaking no-good, useless, gun-toting fools Americans

Canada

These are general slanguage phrases heard everywhere in Canada. You can find slanguage specific to Canadian cities throughout this chapter.

Nickname The Can is our preferred nickname.

Most popular phrase Any phrase ending in "eh" or "A" is a good Canadian phrase. We also mispronounce words such as couch (say coach) or slouch (say slow'ch). We do this merely to annoy Americans.

Famous local food We have no problem with a two-four a day (a case of beer to Americans).

Well-known spot The Semen Tower and the Scrotum Dome are two famous Toronto landmarks.

Popular sport/leisure We live and die hockey. It's pronounced Hoe KEY in Quebec. Pronounce that province Kay BECK.

MISCELLANEOUS SLANGUAGE

Eh or A signifies end of every sentence
You American A major insult to any Canadian
The Peg Winnipeg, Manitoba, Canada
Two-four A case of beer
Tuke or Toque hat
Gitch underwear

Quincy fishing shack

Oh fence something Canadian football teams know little about

Winterpeg Winnipeg

TO Toronto

Scarb suburbanite from Scarborough, Ontario

The Sue Sault Sainte Marie, Ontario

The Can our country

Keep yer stick on the ice Pay attention.

Puck bunny a hockey groupie

Moonies Canadian two-dollar coins

Canuck someone from Canada

Seein' the governor drinking rum

May two-four Weekend Queen Victoria's birthday (accompanied by cases of two-four beer)

The Basketweave Highway 401 across the top of Toronto

Queen Mum Queen Mother

Lotusland what Canadians call Vancouver

The Garage GM Place, where the Canucks play

What a boot me? What about me?

Hogtown Toronto

The Rock what everyone calls the Island of Newfoundland, a province in Canada.

Oon Paipsi May West sil te play the typical Kebecer's breakfast: a Pepsi and a small, cream-filled chocolate cake, for those on the run (*Une Pepsi Mae-West, s'il te plait*)

"Two-Five-Two-Five, We 'ave a wienner!" crazy car dealer commercial, both on French and English TV, that anybody ten and older knows by heart.

Scarberia what southern Torontonians call Scarborough, Ontario

Chesterfield a couch or sofa

Eves trough rain gutter on a house

TTC Toronto Transit Commission (buses, trains, streetcars) in Toronto

Dublin, Ireland

Most popular phrase What's the crack? means How's things? It has nothing to do with a drug.

Famous local food A blonde in a black skirt is a Guinness Stout.

Popular sport/leisure Americans say soccer, but we know it's really football.

There are a few ways to order a Guinness Stout, the lifeblood of Ireland.

A blonde in a black skirt
The Black Stuff
A pint of Arthur
A home and away is a Murphy's and a Guinness

MISCELLANEOUS SLANGUAGE

Is it yourself, Sean? Good morning, Sean.

Lassie girl

Are you for flakes? Do you want cereal?

Crack to have a good time

Gobshite a total idiot

Pog mo thoin Kiss my butt.

Eejit fool

Nixer work done under the table

Plonker fool

Cop On have some sense

Rapid groovy

I'm so hungry I could eat the leg of the lamb of Jesus.

Shut yer gob shut up

It was great crack We had a great time (from the Irish *craic*).

It's a soft day it's misty, foggy, drizzly (like most Irish days)

Holliers holidays

Lucy or Balula crazy

I'm gorbed I'm nervous

Giz yer odds? Could you spare some change?

Goosed by the fiends/shades caught by the cops

What's the suss? What's happening?

Jaysus, me back's givin' me curry My back is sore.

Jax toilet

Skanger hooligan

Mot girl

Aye begoff be garra Is that so.

The business/deadly cool or brilliant
How's the form? hello
Dosh money
How's she cuttin'? How are you?
My moth girlfriend
Mulchie country person
Bogger another word for country person
Gargle a pint of beer
Cheesed off angry
Rozzer policeman
Manky something disgusting
I'm scuttered! I'm absolutely drunk!

Glasgow, Scotland

Yir bum's oot a windy You are talking rubbish.
Hold your wheesht Keep quiet.
Hey, Jimmy Used when trying
        to attract a male's attention.
        Every male in Glasgow seems
        to be called Jimmy.
Irn Bru Iron Brew, a famous local
        soft drink famed for its
        magical healing powers,
        e.g., hangovers.
Doon the toon going down to the
        shops
Pieces sandwiches

I'm gettin' a bevvy I'm getting a drink.

She's clatty She's dirty, a mess, etc.

She wiz beelin' She was really mad.

He's a pure eejit He's really stupid.

Ahm awa tae the cludgie I'm away to the toilet.

I'm goin' oot oan the randan I'm going out on a heavy drinking spree.

Yah arrogant English person with a posh accent

Awmaheid—amnerragaentaepitwanawnleekthaagin

Oh, my head—I will never drink that much again.

Hey Neebir Hello neighbor.

Hong Kong, China

If you can speak English, you can speak Fun Cantonese Slanguage. Without even trying, you'll be talking like the locals. You can speak Fun Slanguage because you already know the words. I've rearranged them to come out in another language. Fun Chinese is the easiest language in the world!!

Read the large, English phrase with emphasis on the ALL CAPS word. Say the phrase quickly yet smoothly. Believe it or not, you're speaking another language. The translations follow. At the bottom of page 142, you'll find pictures that I call moronic devices. Use these pictures to help you pronounce and memorize phrases.

We should have been learning it this way all along. Slanguage is the beginning of the end of language barriers.

Joe sun Good morning.
Neigh hoe ma? How are you?
Hoe fine
Hoe hoe hoe very well
Ma ma who who so so
Hoe Juan ah It's great fun.
Yacht, yee, sum, say, mmm, look, chut one, two, three, four, five, six, seven
Tie Tie wife
May May little sister
Baba father
Hoe pa very afraid
Dick see taxi
Bussy a bus

This section dedicated to Tom, Joannie, Taylor and Lexi King.

Johannesburg, South Africa

Most popular phrase "Howzit my bru?" is a greeting heard here every day.
Famous local food Mampoer is an enjoyable alcohol/peach schnapps.

> Howzit my bru, are the foamies cooking or what today? We
> hit a banker but na, it's cool.
>   Hello buddy, aren't the waves cool today? We hit a sand
> bank, but no worries.

Well-known spot We hang out at the tuckshop, a café to
  most.

Popular sport/leisure While golfing, watch out for lion alerts.
  Lions, some not afraid of man, will venture out on the
  course from time to time. You better boogie up the
  tower to safety!

MISCELLANEOUS SLANGUAGE

Jusnow in a few minutes (up to a half hour)

Cozzie bathing suit

Tackies running shoes or sneakers

Dop tot of liquor

Ag all-purpose exclamation implying irritation, resignation
  or pleasure

I skeem so I think that . . .

Lightie young guy

Bounce us the ages Do you have the time?

Howzit hello

Kak not well

Poppie any female

Biltong dry and salted meat

Tot scenes good-bye (*totsiens* in Afrikaans)

S'corp, skit and honor literally "kick, shoot and thunder," a
curse (skop, skiet en don(d)er)

Lekkers soos 'n' krekker very nice

Hey oaks, we gonna have a lank kif jol Hey, guys, we are going
to have a very cool party.

Kugle and Boer classes of people

Robot traffic light

Tune your cherrie tell your girlfriend

Jammie car

Boney motorbike

Dutchman Afrikaaner

Toppie and Tannie Mom and Dad

Boetie little brother

When-we a returned expatriate (when we were in Canada . . .)

Budgie fly

Dag food

Chin-chwas flirting

Dizzy sleepy

Kiff good

Sarth Efrika South Africa

Yusses Jesus

Ladner, British Columbia, Canada

MISCELLANEOUS SLANGUAGE

Slurry Surrey, British Columbia
Aaaaaaaabottsford (sounds like a sheep) Abbotsford, British Columbia
Poco Port Coquitlam, British Columbia
UBC University of a Billion Chinese
The Coke the Kokahala Highway
Icky-Bicky ICBC (Insurance Corporation of British Columbia—car insurance)

Liverpool, England

Most popular phrase If someone says "I'll burst you," you'd better run.
Well-known spot the homes of the Beatles

MISCELLANEOUS SLANGUAGE

Cracking the flags sunny day
Pure good
Crew gang

Shadin' in pushing in

Bang on mean

Legged chased

Antwacky old-fashioned in a
    derogatory sense

By gum and By 'eck exclamations
    of surprise

Chord mood

Chordy moody

Hangin' unattractive, nasty

Mardy someone easily upset or scared

Meff Idiot

Ronk bad smell

Scrike to cry

Scrikey tearful

Slummy loose change

Smeg-head an imbecile or unliked person, from telly show
    Red Dwarf

Lah guy

Judy girl

Jigger back alley

I'll burst you I'll beat the hell out of you.

Puddled stupid

Corporation pop city drinking water

The Ould Man the father

The Ould Queen the mother

Pulled her on like a wet sock had sex

Scally rogue, juvenile deliquent

THE BEATLES WERE HERE

London, England

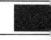

Most popular phrase "May I pinch your seat?" isn't someone trying to be fresh. It means, May I borrow your chair?

Famous local food Fish and chips is the best thing going in London. Yummy, greasy fish and French fries served in newspaper.

Well-known spot Go see the Queen Mum, but don't shake her hand.

Popular sport/leisure When we make a cup of tea, it might be called mashing.

MISCELLANEOUS SLANGUAGE

That's the badger That's wonderful.

Grin on you making fun of

Tube (sometimes pronounced "chube") London subway

Busking bumming for money

Shutcher gob Keep your mouth shut.

Love sir or madam

That's crackin' cool or neat

Quidnunk newsstand attendant

Speng fool

Raggle blatant

Mullet 1980s remnant hairstyle (long at the back and short on top) still commonly seen in Germany

Keep yer pecker up Keep your chin up.

Just because Americans speak English doesn't mean that Americans and the British understand each other. Just try listening to Benny Hill for a bloody second. Here are a few phrases you'll hear in England that might scare you in America.

Gotta fag? Do you have a cigarette?
Got any rubbers? Do you have a pencil eraser?
He pinched yer nuts? Did he steal your cashews?

Plummy dull, boring, stupid

Suspenders woman's garter belt

Braces suspenders (to hold up trousers)

Blank to ignore someone (teen slang)

Alright? Cockney slang for good morning, evening, how are you?

Nicked stolen

Shtoom, Shtoom Muvver Quiet, quiet mother—said in Cockney slang when something embarrassing in the media or in conversation should be censored due to young viewers.

Take the mick to mock or embarrass someone

Bubble and squeak leftover cabbage and mashed potatoes fried in squares in a frying pan and served as an evening meal

Mind the gap Watch your step (heard in the subway).

Watcha What are you doing? (Hello)

Porkie to lie

Pillok idiot

Wrap it up check your fly

Manila, Philippines

Gets moe? Do you understand?
Bababa ba? Is this elevator going down?
Bababa. Yes, going down.
See are restroom (comfort room)
El Are Tee the elevated train system
Hey Joe foreigner
Presidentiable presidential candidate
Erap the current president, Joseph Estrada
Talking Dollars speaking English

Melbourne, Australia

Shout the drinks buy a round of drinks
Cobber a real friend, or mate
Up a gumtree in difficulties
White maggott umpires wear white in
    Australian rules football.
Dunny toilet
Grouse really good

When in Melbourne, pronounce their town MEL bin.
You'll sound like a tourist if you say MEL born.

Slip a yonnie in ya ging and shoot a few spidgies Put a stone in your slingshot and shoot a few sparrows.

Montreal, Quebec, Canada

Nicknames Mun tree awl, Maury al, the most beautiful city in the world

Most popular phrase "Ouest is west, right?" This is the most commonly heard phrase from Anglophone visitors here.

Famous local food Poo TEEN is fries with gravy and lotsa cheese in a big Styrofoam cup.

Well-known spot The dep is the corner store. Comes from deppaneur in French.

Popular sport/leisure Le hoe KEY is king here (French for hockey).

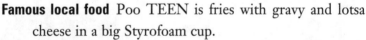

MISCELLANEOUS SLANGUAGE

Hot dog all dress a hot dog with everything
Bazoo old rusted car
Boy, that sure is some good really great
Get oat scram
Green onions the guys who give parking tickets
Mc DO how French people say McDonald's

Canuck a Canadian

Pogo stick corn dog

Eh? or Eh! equivalent to the American "huh." A common phrase ending.

New fee a native of Newfoundland. Also can be used as a derogatory phrase, as in, "What a Newfie, eh?"

Otto root autoroute, highway, interstate, motorway

PEE kist a Québec separatist

More ree AL (French version) Montréal

Hoe KEY almost a religion; a huge passion

Lay Can Nad Dee Ainz les Canadiens, a.k.a. God

Oon bun bee AIR a good beer

Moscow, Russia

If you can speak English, you can speak Russian Slanguage. Without even trying, you'll be talking like the locals. You can speak Fun Slanguage because you already know the words. I've rearranged them to come out in another language.

Read the large, English phrase with emphasis on the ALL CAPS word. Say the phrase quickly yet smoothly. Believe it or not, you're speaking another language. The translations follow. At the bottom of page 142, you'll find pictures that I call moronic devices. Use these pictures to help you pronounce and memorize phrases.

We should have been learning it this way all along. Slanguage is the beginning of the end of language barriers.

Pre vet hello
SPA see bah thank you
Soup me cot YELL lee bee I'd like some soup.
VOE she vegetables
Skolka? How much?
Pa sport passport
Bee'll yet ticket
Vodka vodka

Munich, Germany

If you can speak English, you can speak German Slanguage. Without even trying, you'll be talking like the locals.

Read the large, English phrase with emphasis on the ALL CAPS word. Say the phrase quickly yet smoothly. Believe it or not, you're speaking another language. The translations follow. At the bottom of page 142, you'll find pictures that I call moronic devices. Use these pictures to help you pronounce and memorize phrases.

We should have been learning it this way all along. Slanguage is the beginning of the end of language barriers.

GOO ten tock Good day (*Guten tag*).
Vee GAY tess? How are you? (*Wie geht es?*)
VEE tess sane See you later (*Wiedersehen*).
Shin NECK in snails (*Schnecken*)
Inns Munchin in Munich (*Ins Munich*)
In nine nocked local at the bar (*In ein Nachtlokal*)
Inns KEY no at the movies (*Ins Kino*)
Inns HOE tell to the hotel (*Ins hotel*)
Gift poison (*gift*)
You BELL kite I'm sick (*übelkeit*)
DEEP thief (*Dieb*)
Nine no (*nein*)

Nairobi, Kenya

If you can speak English, you can speak Swahili Slanguage. Without even trying, you'll be talking like the locals. You an speak Fun Slanguage because you already know the words. I've rearranged them to come out in another language.

Read the large, English phrase with emphasis on the ALL CAPS word. Say the phrase quickly yet smoothly. Believe it or not, you're speaking another language. The translations follow. At the bottom of page 142, you'll find pictures that I call moronic devices. Use these pictures to help you pronounce and memorize phrases.

We should have been learning it this way all along. Slanguage is the beginning of the end of language barriers.

Jumbo Hello (*Jambo*).
VP? What's up? (*VP?*)
Cob BOMB bay super (*Kabambe*)
Twain day Let's go (*Twende*).
Knee YACHT tee water buffalo (*Nyati*)
He knee KNEE knee? What's that? (*Hii ni nini?*)
FEE see hyena (*fisi*)
PEE lee PEE lee pepper (*pilipili*)

Newfoundland, Canada

NEW fin lynn Newfoundland
Buy boy (at end of sentence)
Heggs for breakfast? Eggs for breakfast?
NEW fees people from Newfoundland
Ern? Catch any fish?
Nern No, none.
Dapster incompetent person
Whore's eggs sea urchins

Streel messy person

Baywops derogatory term for the people of rural Newfoundland

Shag it b'y, what odds? Forget it, who cares?

Ottawa, Ontario, Canada

Cuffy butt of a cigarette

Deezz dirty person

Oh See (OC) Ottawa-Carleton transportation system. Apparently world class, yet the slowest running in the world.

The Canal the Rideau Canal waterway. Easily converts into the world's longest skating rink.

Beaver tails a very fattening flat-dough pastry topped off with brown sugar and lemon juice, among other things

The Lude winter festival that celebrates our great canal and how much fun it is to freeze our butts off while skating it

The Hill our parliament buildings

Hull our Quebec bordering region

Paris, France

If you can speak English, you can speak French Slanguage. Without even trying, you'll be talking like the locals. You can speak Fun Slanguage because you already know the words. I've rearranged them to come out in another language.

Read the large, English phrase with emphasis on the ALL CAPS word. Say the phrase quickly yet smoothly. Believe it or not, you're speaking another language. The translations follow. At the bottom of page 142, you'll find pictures that I call moronic devices. Use these pictures to help you pronounce and memorize phrases.

We should have been learning it this way all along. Slanguage is the beginning of the end of language barriers.

Bun WE good night (*bonne nuit*)

We say BOW Yes, that's beautiful (*Oui, c'est beau*).

Eel Fay SHOW The weather's warm (*Il fait chaud*).

Sank, cease, set, wheat 5, 6, 7, 8 (*cinq, six, sept, huit*)

Eel say KEY He knows who (*Il sait qui*).

Say may TODD these methods (*ces methodes*)

Kelly Day What an idea (*Quel idée*).

Say dee fee SEAL It's difficult (*C'est difficile*).

Key? Who? (*Qui?*)

Oh cooney Day no idea (*aucune idée*)

Set Tune Bunny Day That's a good idea (*C'est une bonne idée*).

Eel am lay goose DIE He likes garlic bulbs (*Il aime les gousses d'ail*).

Say moose TEAK these mosquitoes (*ces moustiques*)

Two TWO little dog (*toutou*)

Rio de Janeiro, Brazil

If you can speak English, you can speak Portuguese Slanguage. Without even trying, you'll be talking like the locals. You can speak Fun Slanguage because you already know the words. I've rearranged them to come out in another language.

Read the large, English phrase with emphasis on the ALL CAPS word. Say the phrase quickly yet smoothly. Believe it or not, you're speaking another language. The translations follow. At the bottom of page 142, you'll find pictures that I call moronic devices. Use these pictures to help you pronounce and memorize phrases.

We should have been learning it this way all along. Slanguage is the beginning of the end of language barriers.

Comb oh VIE? How's it going? (*Como vai?*)

Bang fine (*bem*)

May NO may . . . My name is (*Meu nome e . . .*)

COMB oh say FALL ah . . . ? How do you say . . . ? (*Como se fala . . . ?*)

Tang SO pa? Do you have soup? (*Tem sopa?*)
A mag KNEE fee co That's magnificent (*E magnifico*)
OH knee booze the bus (*ônibus*)
TOCK see taxi (*taxi*)
OK? What? (*O quê?*)

Rome, Italy

If you can speak English, you can speak Italian Slanguage. Without even trying, you'll be talking like the locals. You can speak Fun Slanguage because you already know the words. I've rearranged them to come out in another language.

Read the large, English phrase with emphasis on the ALL CAPS word. Say the phrase quickly yet smoothly. Believe it or not, you're speaking another language. The translations follow. At the bottom of page 142, you'll find pictures that I call moronic devices. Use these pictures to help you pronounce and memorize phrases.

We should have been learning it this way all along. Slanguage is the beginning of the end of language barriers.

Chow hello or good-bye (*ciao*)
Chow TWO tee hello, everybody (*ciao tutti*)
Bone GOOSE toe a loose translation is "enjoy" (*buon gusto*)

COMB messed ah? How are you? (*Come sta?*)

MOLE toe benny Very well (*Molto bene*).

COMB mess see key AH ma? What's its name? (*Come si chiama?*)

Bell LEE see moe attractive (*bellisimo*)

Kay said EACH? What do you say? (*Che se dice?*)

No MOLE toe not much (*no molto*)

Ah doe MA knee See you tomorrow (*A domani*).

Dell eat see OWES ah delicious (*deliziosa*)

Chow, belly hello (or good-bye), handsome men (*Ciao, belli*)

Saskatoon, Saskatchewan, Canada

Stoon Saskatoon

Toon Town Saskatoon

Saskabush Saskatoon or Saskatchewan

Tee Bay Thunder Bay, Ontario

The Dub WHL (Western Hockey League)

Rezbians University students who live "in rez" (the dorms)

Seoul, South Korea

If you can speak English, you can speak Korean Slanguage. Without even trying, you'll be talking like the locals. You can speak Fun Slanguage because you already know the words. I've rearranged them to come out in another language.

Read the large, English phrase with emphasis on the ALL CAPS word. Say the phrase quickly yet smoothly. Believe it or not, you're speaking another language. The translations follow. At the bottom of page 142, you'll find pictures that I call moronic devices. Use these pictures to help you pronounce and memorize phrases.

We should have been learning it this way all along. Slanguage is the beginning of the end of language barriers.

An young Good morning.
Oh so please
Comb mop sum kneed ah Thank you.
Tongue gun chew say oh? May I have carrots?
Bong chew say oh? May I have bread?
Oh new choke? Which one?
Cop she'd ah Let's go.

Sydney, Australia

Nicknames Oz, A stray ya

Most popular phrase "Look, mate, she went off her face and spit the dummy." This translates as, "You know, buddy, she went a bit crazy and threw a tantrum."

Famous local food Foster's, 'Strine for beer

Well-known spot Anyplace here is beautiful, as long as you avoid the man-eating crocs and sharks.

Popular sport/leisure We love to surf, with or without clothing. Anybody who is new to this might be called a shark biscuit.

MISCELLANEOUS SLANGUAGE

True blue a real Australian

Blue person with red hair

Bonza a good time

Fair suck of the sav, luv Oh, for Heaven's sake.

That's grass That's cool.

Billabong wet lagoon

Jackaroo male station hand

Jilleroo female station hand

'Strine or Stray an what we speak

Septic American

Sandgroper someone from Western Australia

Lamington traditional cake; it's a sponge with chocolate icing covering it. If asked if you would like a cuppa and a lamington, say, "Yes, please."

Logi award won by Aussie television personalities

Darryl crispy end of a cooked sausage roll

Tucker food

Joe Bloggs John Doe

Lemon smash lemonade

Lemonade Sprite, 7 Up, etc.

Eighteenth of the tenth October 18

Dummy pacifier (that an infant sucks on)

Hungry Jack's Burger King

Nappies diapers

Sultana banana

Cabbage air head

Pikelets (PIKE lets) silver dollar pancakes

Mollydooker left-hander

Tokyo, Japan

If you can speak English, you can speak Japanese Slanguage. Without even trying, you'll be talking like the locals. You can speak Fun Slanguage because you already know the words. I've rearranged them to come out in another language.

Read the large, English phrase

with emphasis on the ALL CAPS word. Say the phrase quickly yet smoothly. Believe it or not, you're speaking another language. The translations follow. At the bottom of page 142, you'll find pictures that I call moronic devices. Use these pictures to help you pronounce and memorize phrases.

We should have been learning it this way all along. Slanguage is the beginning of the end of language barriers.

Ohio goes Imus Good morning (*ohayo gozaimus*).

Cone KNEE chee wah Good day (*konnichi wa*).

Comb Bun Wah Good evening (*komban wa*).

Mushy Mushy Hello (on the telephone) (*moshi moshi*).

Cuda sigh please (*kudasai*)

Toe moe dutchy friend (*tomodachi*)

Guy jean foreigner (*gaijin*)

Tie hen joe zoo dess You're very good (talented) (*Taihenjozu desu*).

Knee hone Japan (*nihon*)

Knee hone go Japanese (*nihongo*)

A notta wah ski dess I like you (*Anatawa suki des*).

Comb pie to your health (*Compai*)

Toronto, Ontario, Canada

Nicknames Cabbagetown, Big Smoke, Tee oh, Tee dot, Tee dot oh dot

Most popular phrase "How 'boat a pop?" means would you like a soda?

Famous local food We drink a brand of milk called Homo milk. It has nothing to do with our sexual preferences.

Well-known spot S & M Club. It's a club full of people from the suburbs (Scarborough and Mississauga).

Popular sport/leisure Riding the Vomit Comet is a nighttime pursuit of many. This bus runs all night from downtown to the suburbs and transports those who are too drunk to drive.

MISCELLANEOUS SLANGUAGE

Beaver tail small pancake-like pastry with lemon and brown sugar

The gist and the pist federal and provincial taxes in Ontario (GST and PST)

Four Oh One Highway 401 (call it anything else, and you're wrong)

'Shwa borough of Oshawa

Torontonian someone from Toronto, Ontario. Derogatory to everyone except Torontonians. Don't ask me why!

American calling any Torontonian one is an insult.

CPP Canada Pension Plan

OHIP Ontario Health Insurance Plan (pronounced Oh-Hip)

The Semen Tower and the Scrotum Dome famous Toronto landmarks

BAG Uls bagels, to those who live in Sault Ste. Marie

The Jolly Green Giant's urinal the new city hall

Canadian money something worth 35 cents less everywhere else

Canuck buck Canadian dollars

Click a kilometer (1.6 kilometers per mile for you U.S. people)

Sixty pounder 60-ounce bottle of booze

Vancouver, British Columbia, Canada

Bite moose Go away.

Oat in a boat Out and about.

Brollywood Vancouver nickname

Overtown over Vancouver to North Vancouver

Eavestrough that thing your water runs down the side of your house in

Surrey girls the women who dress easy in Surrey, British Columbia

Sky Train light-rail transit system

SeaBus boat transit system

The Echodome BC Place Stadium during a rock concert

The Garage GM Place, where the Canucks and Grizzlies lose . . . er, play their home games

The Island Vancouver Island

The marshmallow in bondage BC Place Stadium

The Tube the George Massey Tunnel, which goes under the south arm of the Fraser River

Vancouver rain festival occurs from September 1 through August 31

Winnipeg, Manitoba, Canada

Nickname Winterpeg

Well-known spot "The Falls" is short for Yosemite Falls. All other waterfalls are called by their first names: Bridal veil, Vernal, Nevada or Horsetail.

Popular sport/leisure Bearproofing is what you must do if you don't want your stuff ravaged by a brown bear.

MISCELLANEOUS SLANGUAGE

Tioga Tioga Pass, the quickest route from Yosemite to Nevada and points east. "Opening Tioga" is the springtime occupation of the snowplow drivers.

The River Canyon the section of the highway (and the surrounding terrain) going into Yosemite from Mariposa on Highway 140, with the Merced River running through it. This is the WORST place to get stuck behind a touron (tourist + moron). Very scenic; also very dangerous.

El Cap, El Capitan, El Cap Meadow the meadow in front of El Capitan

The Village Yosemite Village, the residential/shopping area inside the park. Also a serious tourist hangout.

The Lodge Yosemite Lodge

The Caf the cafeteria at Yosemite Lodge

The Ahwahnee the Ahwahnee Hotel

Cockney Rhyming Slanguage

Cockney Rhyming Slanguage is very popular in all English-speaking countries except for America.

Up the apple and pears stairs

Bag of fruit suit

Lug hole ear

Bum rag newspaper

Cobber mate

Get stuffed get ******

Full as a doctor's wallet drunk

Brahms & List pissed

Mutton & Geoff deaf

Dead horse tomato sauce

Fair dinkum the truth

Ridgey didge for real

Dog's eye　meat pie

China plate　my best mate (someone of value to you, as a boy-friend, girlfriend, wife, hubby)

Tin lids　kids (children)

Joe blake　snake

Sky rocket　pocket

Okker pringer　finger

Rubber de dub　the bathtub

Ham and eggs　legs (also known as poles)

Boat race　face (also known as Oxford & Cambridge)

Whistle & flute　cute (also known as Whistle)

Richard the Third　what you do in the toilet (also known as Richard)

Jack and Jills　pills (tablets, not bills)

Suzie Wongs　thongs

It's all gone a bit Pete Tong　basically means that it's gone wrong

Trouble and strife　wife

GENeRAtionAL SLANGuage

1) **Praise the Lord and pass the ammunition.**
2) **Jumpin jive**
3) **Let's remember Pearl Harbor.**
4) **The royal family of Swing:**
     Benny Goodman, The King
     Duke Ellington, The Duke
     Count Basie, The Count
     Ella Fitzgerald, The Queen
     Frank Sinatra, The Chairman of the Board

Neat!

Kookie, Kookie, lend me your comb.

Nukular bum

That's George! (late forties to early fifties) That's really nice.

Boss

Submarine races

Foam domes stuffed bra

Beatnik counterculture precursor to "hippie," coined by columnist Herb Caen

Cool cat

Nifty

Keen

Swell

Tailfins

Hoopskirt

Hep cat

Daddy-O

Bug out! Korean War vintage, meaning Get the h*** out of here!

How sweet it is! Jackie Gleason catchphrase that caught on

And awayyyyy we go! another Jackie Gleasonism

Sit ins These started in the 1950s, not during the college antiwar demonstrations of the 1960s, and for a much more honorable reason, namely, civil rights.

Cherry popular term around 1957 meaning great, really neat, etc.

Cheesecake what to call your girlfriend, kind of like "sweetie"

Doo rag a scarf you put over your hairdo to help it set or protect it when you sleep (males and females)

Conk from Congolene, a chemical preparation used to straighten hair (afterward you put on your doo rag so that it sets up properly)

Kicks shoes

Threads clothing

George a dollar bill

Pad home or apartment

Dufus a stupid person or lacking in social skills

Lid hat

Mickey Mouse a watch, as in, "Check Mickey, we're late."

Dipstick light in the IQ department

Dinch to put out a cigarette
Grease to eat
Shoot the breeze to converse
Square
Sock hop
Gee whiz
Golly jeepers
Holy crumb
Don't that irk ya?
Liften, cliffin
Big deal
Holy cow
Oh, gosh

1960s

"Keep on truckin'!"
Flower power
Hip
That's totally trippy
Heavy, man
Bummer
Matchbox (of grass)
Bad trip
Rip off
Score get some dope
Rap to talk
Get clean for Gene Eugene McCarthy

Chicago Seven
Yippies
Far out
Apple pie makes you sterile
Mary Poppins was a junkie
Right on
Uptight
Outta sight
Bum rap
What a trip
Psychedelic
Say good night, Dick
Let it all hang out
Here come da judge (popularized by the TV show *Laugh-In*)
Sock it to me (popularized by the TV show *Laugh-In*)
You bet your sweet bippy (popularized by the TV show *Laugh-In*)
War is not healthy for children and other living things
Hippies
High
Mind-bending
The Man anyone representing the establishment
Peacenik
Alice B. Toklas brownies brownies w/marijuana baked in
"Danger, Will Robinson"

1970s

"Hang in there!"
"You've come a long way, baby."
Leisure suits
Who's your favorite in the *Brady Bunch*?
Disco, Disco Duck
YMCA
Do the Hustle
Please don't squeeze the Charmin
Wild and crazy guy

Up ya nose wid a rubba hose
Nanu, nanu
I'm Chevy Chase and you're not
"I can't believe I ate the WHOLE thing."
Try it, you'll like it Alka Seltzer commercial
Hold the pickle, hold the lettuce Burger King commercial
Earth shoes
Puzzle rings, mood rings
What's your sign? Zodiac
Tricky Dick Richard Nixon
Dyn-o-mite! JJ Walker
Bra-burners feminists
Aaaaaayyyy! the Fonz
"Sit on it!" also the Fonz
Shake your booty
Let's boogie
Funky
Bicentennial Minute

1980s

"Where's the beef?"
Totally rad
Sooo gnarly
Bogus, dude
Voodoo economics
Trickle-down theory
Like, oh my God
I want my MTV
Don't worry, be happy
No respect
Gag me with a spoon
Awesome
"You look mahvelous!"
Val-speak
Chill out
Totally tubular
Drug czar
"Rock on!"
Grotey

1990s

Teflon president
"You go, girl!"
"Uhhh, shut up, Beavis."

Word up

Been there, done that

Not!

"Life is like a box of chocolates . . . "

Bin dare, done dat

Hellow-o-o???? Don't you get it? Are you listening?

You the man

Whoop, there it is

Bite me

Like, you know

Gettin' jiggy with it

Skanky

Skankadelic

As if!

Whatever!

Kurt Cobain

Like I care!

"Here's a quarter, call someone who cares."

Sick later nineties equivalent of the overused "Cool"

Grrls

Riot grrls

Spin doctor

Go postal

"Ehh, Macarena!"

Fusion cooking

Garbage plate cooking

TEENAGE SLANGuage

Teen slanguage of the nineties is difficult to understand. I think that's why I like it so much. I hope today's teens don't get mad if their parents buy this book and can suddenly understand what their teenage kids are saying.

Get your mack on flirt with someone

Freal dough I am in total agreement!

Socs or the pops socials or "the populars," in other words, the popular kids and the social kids, which are really the same thing

Mack daddy guy who gets all the girls

Boulder dork

Butters awesome (to describe)

Groovy tomato really neat or cool. . . .

Get jiggy dress up so that you are very attractive

Goo! Oh my God

Smell ya bye

Schnit! Dang!

Gimpdog friend

The jam when something's really cool

That guy is mmm-mmm good or **That guy is Campbell's soup**

Wha the dilly? What up? How are things?

Krunk to make things get wild

dope cool

Off tha hooks really cool

Crashy foul, out of line, messed up, etc.

Let's roll let's go

Peacin' out leaving

Bouncin' leaving

What's up, home-dog-skillet? What's up, boys?

Ferreal B? Seriously, friend?

Gravy groovy

Mashed potatoes a reply to gravy

YO Cuz, that jank be bonk, homey G Hey cousin, that thing is
     weird, brother.

My bad I apologize

Crescent fresh cool, neato

That's chewy that's cool; that's interesting

Forsheezy for sure

Wankbiscuit a wannabee, a follower

Whomp this is really not fair

Brick cold

Chillin' like a villain hanging out

Mad skizzillz great talents

Don't get stank I don't want that attitude

Turkey disco jivin' (used as an adjective or a verb) the greatest
person, or cool

Dopey fresh tight y'all that's cool

Yo, that bird was bomb digity that girl was good-looking

Lights are on! parents are in the room

Trippin' doing something stupid

GTG, g2g got to go

Fundork your best friend

Vern psycho

Toolbox dork or geek

Choad another dork or geek

Fargus darn it, as in, "Fargus, I forgot to shut off my light!"

The sick bomb better than the bomb, as in, "But, dude. We
were kickin' it at my house. My parents are in Fresno. It
was the sick bomb!"

The sick atomic bomb even better than the sick bomb

Ghetto unfair

TELeVISion SLANGuage

SATURDAY NIGHT LIVE

In the seventies, everybody spoke like the characters on this show.

Samurai Night Fever John Belushi's sketch
Ohhhh Kayyyyy what Steve Martin said
Bass-o-matic Dan Aykroyd's commercial
Baba Wawa Gilda Radner's rendition of Barbara Walters
Never mind Emily Letella's sign-off
Gonna get me a shotgun, and shoot all you whiteys Garrett Morris's line in a prison skit
I'm Gumby, dammit Eddie Murphy's takeoff on Gumby
Mr. Bill Play-Doh figure that always got killed in skits
Pat the androgenous one
I, I BUH We, Bah firty fee, New Nork, New Nork Eddie Murphy's Buckwheat dialog (from *Little Rascals*)
"We are two wild and crazy guys." Martin/Aykroyd as two Czech brothers
Cheeseburger, cheeseburger, Pepsi, Pepsi, Pepsi famous skit in Chicago deli

ALL IN THE FAMILY

Seven hundred faw how's a 704 Hauser Street
Hem a rude hemmoroid

The blessing menstrual period
A visit from her friend menstrual period
Cronkite's a Commie
Little goyle Archie's daughter
    Gloria
Chrome a stones chromo-
    somes
Tootie sweety French for "right
    away"
We moan sewer French for "yes, sir"
Pour some more Spanish for please
Maudie's here something Archie hated to hear (when his
    sister-in-law visited)
Homosapiens are killer fags what Archie thought

GILLIGAN'S ISLAND

Poolu see bah goomba Gilligan's attempt to speak like the
    natives
G-I-Double L-I-G-A-N spells Gilligan song derived from
    "Harrigan"
Erika Tiffany Smith a visitor to their
    island
Harold HECK you bah An
    obnoxious director/
    producer who was
    stranded temporar-
    ily on their island

> Blanket, blanket, on the shelf
> Come to Gilligan by yourself

Lord Beasley butterfly scientist
Eva Grubb another visitor to their island. Great name.
It's a bird, it's a plane, it's Super Gilligan.

SEINFELD

Guess which character said these phrases on arguably the funniest TV show ever.

He's in da batroom (Elaine's dad)
Mulva (George and Jerry)
Eiffel Towers (Mr. Seinfeld)
Can't stand ya (George's gym teacher)
Todd Gakk (Elaine)
Flush twice (Jerry)
LAY knee (Jerry)
Dr. Van Nostrin (Kramer)
Tippy toe, tippy toe (George)
Mob'll Roy (an old lady)

> **I'M OUT**
> —Kramer

Poppy pee'd (Jerry)

His whole life is a fantasy camp (George)

Significant shrinkage (George)

Kill me now, I'm begging you (George)

Things are creakin' and crackin' (Jerry)

Welcome to Movie Phone (Kramer)

I don't like this thing, and here's what I'm doing with it (Elaine)

Shmoopie (Jerry and his girlfriend)

Pity is very underrated (George)

I'm incapable of guile (George)

Haitian voodoo wacko torture (Mr. Peterman)

Can't handle a little spice? (Elaine's dad)

FRIENDS

Viva Las GAY Gas Chandler's dad's show

Your nipular region is showing.

You were gonna drink the fat what Ross was going to do to show his love to Rachel

You licked the spoon? Joey's habit

Dr. Drake Remore Joey's character on a soap

Roy Gooblie Monica's date to the prom

I'm gonna kick Chip's ass what Monica's date said when their plans almost got canceled

---

Hey, the pages are stuck together.
CHANDLER!!!

Ride the Tube in London What Monica and Ross's father mentioned to their mother. She thought it was something sexual they did.

MARY TYLER MOORE

TBFBS Ted Baxter's Famous Broadcast School

Let it soak, Mare what Rhoda said to Mary about the overflowing dishes in the sink

Good nice and have a pleasant newt Ted Baxter's sign-off

Requiem for a peanut fictitious title for Chuckle the Clown's final chapter in life

WJM where they worked

Happy Homemaker Sue Anne Nivens, the happy, easy host of this show

MARRIED WITH CHILDREN

Cluck You what Al said to Marcy the chicken

I before E except before E-I-E-I-O Kelly's spelling helper

Case a rum how Kelly speaks French

Co winky dink Kelly's attempt at coincidence

Listen, missy Marcy's response to her husband, Jefferson

Grand Master B Bud's moniker

> **Shoe Groupie** The female who loved Al

NO MA'AM Men Against Amazonian Masterhood
Circular incision what Al's operation should have been instead of a circumcision

IN LIVING COLOR

Reading is fallopian Reading is fundamental
You emaciated hermaphrodite, I like a little cream in my coffee what ugly girl said to the vampire
You better stop, Gary Coleman what ugly girl said to the vampire when she thought he was Gary Coleman
I've seen the face of Satan what someone said when they saw under ugly girl's dress
Yo mama's boogers are big as bowling balls phrase from a competition of who can insult each other the best
I'm bi . . . lingual Antoine's statement
Gulp one of Blaine and Antoine's products they endorsed
Hated It! Blaine and Antoine's "Men on Film" judgment
Don't swallow . . . I never do Antoine's statement in his boxing movie
Homey the Clown funny, violent clown played by Damon Wayans
Handi-Man kind of like Superman
Fly Girls dancers

SITCOM SLANGUAGE

This is Carlton your doorman *Rhoda*

Doh! Homer Simpson

Whatchoo talkin' 'bout, Willis? Gary Coleman in *Dif'rent Strokes*

That's a lovely dress you have on, Mrs. Cleaver Eddie on *Leave It to Beaver*

Newman! what Jerry always says when he sees Newman

To the moon, Alice!

One of these days, one of these days—POW!—right in the kisser

Baby, you're the greatest all by Ralph Kramden on *The Honeymooners*

Work? Maynard G. Krebs on *The Many Loves of Dobie Gillis*

I don't fool around, boy Ricky Nelson on *Ozzie and Harriet*

Nussing. I know nussing! Sergeant Schultz on *Hogan's Heroes*

Meathead

Stifle yourself Archie Bunker on *All In the Family*

Holy hole in a doughnut Robin on *Batman*

Sit on it

Ayyyyyy (thumbs up) Fonzie on *Happy Days*

> Same bat time
> Same bat channel

Sorry about that, Chief
Thanks, I needed that
Would you believe . . .   all by Maxwell Smart on *Get Smart*
Nanu, nanu Mork from *Mork and Mindy*
Yum, Yum Herman Munster

Movies

Cool Hand Luke

I can eat fifty eggs Luke's famous challenge
My Lucille woman they all adored, but couldn't have
What we have here is failure to communicate Cap'n's line
What's yer dirt doin' in boss's ditch?
I'm shakin' it, boss heard before Luke left
Babaluga, Koko, Cap'n, Dragline, Blind Dick, Mullet Head other
    characters
Sometimes nothin' is a real cool hand Luke's motto
The sweatiest movie ever made

Kelly's Heroes

Oddball, Kelly, Crapgame, Big Joe main characters
Stop with those negative vibes Oddball's reaction to some-
    thing he doesn't want to hear
Woof woof Oddball's reaction to finding the gold

Cartoons

Only Speed and Scooby merit any recognition here . . . .

Baby Grand Prix the only race that Spritle got to race in

X3 (the Melange) a car that ran by itself

Ooh Speed what Trixie exclaimed when Speed tried something

You'll never find out Racer X's motto

Cruncher Block the owner of the Mammoth Car

X9 Racer X's car number

Inspector Detector their local cop

Dugaree one of Speed's rivals

Snake Oiler another of Speed's rivals

Chim Chim their primate cohort

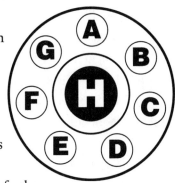

Scooby-Doo

Raggy how Scooby said
  Shaggy
**And I would have got-
    ten away with it,
    too . . . if it hadn't
    been for those
    meddling kids!**
  ended many shows

Scrappy-Doo Scooby's nephew
Scooby-Dum Scooby's cousin

I detested all of Scooby's family members. Let's not
mention any more.

Ruby-Rue Scooby-Doo spoken in his own slanguage
Scooby snack Scooby's rewards
Mystery Machine their transportation
Charlie the Robot a character
Phantom Puppeteer a character
Fred, Daphne, Velma, Shaggy the sleuths
Ruh-roe Uh-oh in Scooby's own slanguage

RANdom SLANGuages

Personal Ads Slanguage

What personal ads really mean.

FEMALE PERSONALS

40-ish 49 and a half

Adventurer has had a lot of sex

Athletic no breasts or butt

Average-looking ugly

Beautiful a liar

Contagious smile has VD

Educated flunked out of college

Emotionally secure takes antidepressants

Feminist pain in the butt

Free-spirited smokes dope

Friendship first easy

Fun annoying

New Age never shaves her legs or armpits

Open-minded desperate

Outgoing loud and obnoxious

Poet depressed

Professional cold

Redhead dyes her hair

Romantic candlelight hides her flaws

Voluptuous very fat

Wants soulmate possible stalker

Widow nagged first husband to death

MALE PERSONALS

40-ish 52 and looking for a young tart

Athletic sits on the couch, watches ESPN and dominates clicker

Average-looking lots of hair in ears and on back

Educated thinks you're an idiot

Free spirit sleeps with your sister

Fun good with a remote and a six-pack

Good-looking conceited

Honest a liar

Huggable fat

Mature impossible

Physically fit stares at himself in mirror

Poet his canvas is bathroom stalls

Stable occasional stalker, but never been caught

Thoughtful says "please" when demanding something

Malapropisms

These are fun because people don't know if you're stupid or just messing with 'em.

He strained his groan muscle (groin)

Don't burn that incest (incense)

According to his last will and testicle (last will and testament)

She's experiencing mental pause (menopause)

The student was suspended for suppository remarks (derogatory remarks)

He delivered the urology (eulogy)

I'm under the consumption (assumption)

Homie Talk Slanguage

Kipykoo Keep it cool.

Hos a da boo House of Blues

Scooby Doo A dog just went on your leg.

Ak m ood Smack them good.

Wha ee oo ay? What did you say?

Squishey excuse me

Yo adjective used for individuals

40 a 40-ounce bottle of beer

Shorty term of endearment, usually for a young person or cute female

Dogg, B, or Homie terms of endearment, usually for guys, among themselves

Trippin', Buggin', or Lunchin' acting irrationally

Spinner DJ (disc jockey)

Diss to disrespect

Gank or jack to steal or mug

Creepin' sneaking to see someone you're not supposed to be seeing, usually in relationships

Crib or lab your home

Da HOOD the neighborhood

Trac an instrumental
Got skillz or game talented in a particular aspect
Headz or peeps groups of people
Madd large quantities, as in "There was madd headz at my crib."
Bounce, ghost, or outtie 5000 to leave the area or scene
Gat or burner (heater) gun
Seed your child
Five oh, one time, or po po the police
Ducketts, endz, or dead presidents cash, money

Kentucky Hillbilly Slanguage

Taters potatoes
Maters home-grown tomatoes
Cornbread fed country boy/girl
Y'all you all
Swappin' trading
Young 'uns kids
Porch monkeys kids
Cats Kentucky Wildcats
Nascar That's a real nice car.
Mammy mother
Pappy father
Uanto? You want to?
Porkin' making love
What's kickin', chicken? What's happening? What's up?
Cuttin' the rug partying

Holler yell, or a valley

Crick creek

Baccer chewing tobacco, tobacco products

Yonder a ways away

Gander look

Crooked neck someone who likes to gander

Ridge the top of a hill, opposite of holler

Hillbilly someone from Kentucky

— © 1999 by Lisa Lacefield Humphrey

SPorts SLANGuage

Sports Nicknames Slanguage

Nicknames are an important part of every sport, probably because they are important to every boy who grows up in America. Here are some nicknames for teams, groups of individuals and teammates.

TEAM NICKNAMES

Broad Street Bullies Philadelphia Flyers hockey team
The Whiz Kids 1950 Philadelphia Phillies baseball team
The Wheeze Kids 1983 Philadelphia Phillies baseball team
Big Red Machine Cincinnati Reds during their dynasty of the
    seventies
Bronx Bombers New York Yankees
The Amazing Mets New York Mets from 1969

Groups within Teams

Purple People Eaters the Minnesota Viking defense during
    the seventies
Gang Green the Philadelphia Eagles defense
Orange Crush Denver Broncos defense

Individuals

Slammin' Sammy Sammy Sosa of the Chicago Cubs
Big Mac Mark McGwire of the St. Louis Cardinals
The Polish Rifle Ron Jawarski of the Philadelphia Eagles
Mr. October Reggie Jackson of the New York Yankees
Round Mound of Rebound Charles Barkley as he was known at
    Auburn
Dr. J Julius Erving of the Philadelphia 76ers
Chocolate Thunder Darryl Dawkins of the Philadelphia 76ers
Hands of Stone Roberto Duran, boxer
Wilt the Stilt Wilt Chamberlain of the Philadelphia 76ers
The Bull Greg Luzinski of the Philadelphia Phillies
Sweetness Walter Payton of the Chicago Bears
The Fridge William Perry of the Chicago Bears
His Airness Michael Jordan of the Chicago Bulls

Baseball Slanguage

Dinger home run
Pearl-ball, rock-ball, cheese fastball
Heater fastball
Rope hard-hit ball
Hanger a weak curveball
Hammer curveball
Bender curveball
Chuck and duck hard-hit ball at the pitcher

Duck fart a weak hit fly ball

Punching Judy a weak hit ground ball

Texas league single a weak hit ground ball

Bomb home run

The dish home plate

Stick bat

Trophy a batter who doesn't swing

Crucifix beanball in the back

Dip tobacco

The corners 1st and 3rd

Lid hat

Boot the ball fielding error

Ribeyes runs batted in

Tater home run

The 1974, 1975 Philadelphia Flyers

The Broad Street Bullies, a rough and tumble hockey team. We loved them. We also loved the games that took four hours and were filled with twelve fights.

God Bless America what Kate Smith always sang

The Hammer Dave Schultz

The Hound Bob Kelly

Moose André Dupont

Broad Street Bullies their favorite nickname. Opponents hated visiting the Spectrum, Spectrum, Spectrum.

Big Bird Don Saleski

Cowboy Bill Flett
Bubby Clarke, eh?
The Fan Tom Bladon
Only the Lord saves move Goalie Bernie Parent

1993 Phillies Slanguage

They won the pennant. They shoulda won the World Series. Their gruff, yet lovable demeanor can be summed up by a headline in one of the Atlanta newspapers that ran as the Phils were visiting Atlanta on their way to the pennant: HIDE YOUR WOMEN AND CHILDREN; THE PHILADELPHIA PHILLIES ARE COMING TO TOWN. We'll never forget them.

Head Dave Hollins
Krukker John Kruk
Dutch Darren Daulton
Icy Jim Eisenrich
Inky Pete Incaviglia
Batman Kim Batiste
Milty Milt Thompson
Schill Curt Schilling
Incredible Hulk Danny Jackson
Wild Thing Mitch Williams
Nails Lenny Dykstra
Tank Todd Pratt

1985 Chicago Bears Slanguage

We are the Bears...

I lived in Chicago for a year just after the Bears won the Super Bowl. A great team in a great city. Lotsa slanguage here besides the Fridge.

Jimmy Mac Jim McMahon (or the punky qb)
Speedy Willie Willie Gault
44–0 crushing defeat of hated Cowboys
Black and Blues Brothers their offensive line
Sweetness Walter Payton
Suey fullback Matt Suey
Buddy defensive coach Buddy Ryan
46D Buddy's pet defense
The Sackman Richard Dent
Samurai Mike Mike Singletary
The Hitman Gary Fencik
Mama's Boy Otis Otis Wilson
The Super Bowl Shuffle their celebratory dance
15–1 their almost perfect record
Ditka God-like coach Mike Ditka

RECreaTIONal SLANGuage

Gambling Slanguage

Pitboss supervisor of a "pit" of tables, e.g., dice pit, 21 pit, etc.

Jackpot a mess of trouble

Sing to call a long sequence of winning dice rolls

George a gambler who tips the dealers well

Flea a person who places small annoying bets

Stroak to purposefully place a complicated bet to annoy the dealer

Bird 25 cents (usually)

Nickel five dollars

Dime ten dollars

Tokes tips

Color to convert odd denominational winnings into an easy to manage handful

Shoe Horseshoe Casino on Fremont

The Riv Riveria Casino

DICE SLANGUAGE

Midnight twelve

Boxcars twelve

Snake eyes two

C and E crap and eleven

Hard ways when the dice are identical (two ones, two twos, etc.)

Flea small-time gambler

Shooter big-time gambler

CRAPS SLANGUAGE

Craps has an entire language of its own. Here are a few terms that can be fun for everyone:

Eyes of a mother-in-law a two (call 'em snake eyes and you're marked as a tourist)

Little Joe a four

Ace-Deuce a three

Yo an eleven

Hard way even numbers rolled in pairs (e.g., hard eight, both dice show fours)

Easy way even numbers rolled other than in pairs (e.g., easy eight, the dice show six and two or three and five)

Twenty-two a hard four

Mom and Pop a hard eight

Square pair a hard eight

Sunflowers a hard ten

For the boys a bet for the dealers (a tip)

Any for a penny a one-dollar "any craps" bet

Bettin' the don't betting against the shooter; can be used for any situation one is pessimistic about

Hot hand a shooter who's making everyone a lot of money

Golf Slanguage

A woody par a hole off a tree

Shoot an Arnie par a hole without hitting the fairway

Sandy par the hole out of a sand trap

Ridiculoft the author's ball-flight pattern

O.B. Gyn out of bounds

Stroke shaver a cheater

Wooder what a Philadelphia golfer avoids

Boyd what a New York golfer desires

Pair what a Chicago golfer would like to shoot

Iggle what a Philadelphia golfer would love to shoot

Annie Palma Arnold Palmer in Boston

Pop, splash, push, Nassau golfers' gambling terms

Bite, bite, bite me often overheard on golf courses

Almighty Higs local Philadelphia-area golfer who hits driver seven 580 yards. Rumor has it that he gives Tiger strokes.

Fat bastard often overheard on the golf course, aka chunky

Addams' Family adjective for a golfer who lurches

U-Haul a golfer with a hitch in their swing

Skateboarding Slanguage

Krispin' cool
Jakish too bad
Way up a high alley-oop
Probs problems with your
        board
Sprinky broken board
The Ollie flip, Pop shove it, K grind
        some maneuvers
Plywood pusher Say this and
        expect to get punched by a skateboarder.
Sk8ers what we are
Bladers who we hate (in-line skaters)
The quest for air what we desire

Skier Slanguage

Yard sale when someone crashes
        on the slopes and their gear
        flies all over the place
Gaper a beginner skier
Grizwalds a family of gapers
Smok'n monkeys a gaper in a race tuck
        and a snowplow
Unguided missile a child going straight down
        with no turns

Mt. Flatular a.k.a. Mt. Bachelor (lack of slope)

Zoo-ed a very crowded run

Surfer Slanguage

Rock Lobster sunburn

Flat and Glassy no surf, or a person with no personality and too much beer, depending on context

The waves were smokin' the waves were big

The waves were epic the waves were huge

He's a kook He's a person who tries to surf and be cool, but surfs bad and is not cool.

Caught some barrels went surfing

Got barrelled surfed in the barrel of a wave

Got dumped The wave crashed on me while I was in it.

Rippin' surfing well

Line-up where all the surfers wait for the waves

Leash line that attaches your board to your ankle

Gun board made for surfing huge waves

Going over the falls when a surfer falls from the top of a wave. Often painful.

Pearling when the front of the board goes underwater. From pearl diving.

Mountain Biking Slanguage

Bacon scabs
Corndog to be covered in silt after a crash
Death cookies small rocks that jar the bike
    and endanger the rider
Digger face-first crash
Granny gear lowest, easiest-to-pedal gear on your bike
Gutter bunny commuter on a bike
John Boy chunks of mud stuck to your face
Potato chip badly bent wheel
Skid lid helmet

Rodeo Slanguage

Spinner rodeo bull that spins more than he bucks
In the well where a bullrider goes on a spinner
Sticky bullrider who has a good average
Salty bullrider with style
He'll check yer dipstick get a horn you know
    where
He's hung rider is thrown, but his foot is still
    stuck in the stirrup
Frappuccino a bull's name
Slam dunk rider who was thrown off with vigor
    by the bull
Bullfighters clowns

Bowling Slanguage

"Hit 'em light and watch 'em fight" a strike on a light hit that bounces the pins around instead of blowing them back into the pit

"No drive, no five" ball that deflects from the head pin, thus failing to take out the #5 pin. A shot without enough power to drive through for a strike.

One-eighty pinsetter that is jammed one-quarter of the way (180 degrees) through its 720 degree cycle.

Bananas pinsetter that becomes jammed after picking up pins, leaving them suspended over the deck like—you guessed it—a bunch of bananas. Also called a banana rack.

Brooklyn ball that crosses to the other side—left of the head pin for right-handers, or right of the head pin for left-handers. Also called a Jersey Squasher.

Bucket four pins left standing in a diamond formation

Bumpers 60-foot-long air bags placed in the gutters for tiny tot bowlers. No gutter balls, guaranteed.

Double dribble ball released too early, making it bounce on the lane

Dutchman; Dutch 200; Dutch deuce 200-game bowled by alternating strikes and spares

Greek Church unusual split with two pins on one side and three on the other—a 4–6–7–8–10 or 4–6–7–9–10. (Why Greek Church? I have no idea.)

Railroad a 4–6–7–10 split. Also called "the big four."

Sandbagger one who deliberately bowls badly to achieve a high handicap for later competition. The lowest form of cheating. (Side note: A "sandbagger" on CB radio is someone who listens for a long time without talking or responding to calls.)

Sleeper a pin "hiding" behind another—8-pin behind the 2-pin, 5-pin behind the head pin, or 9-pin behind the 3-pin. Also called "a man in the bedroom" or "a man in the closet."

Turkey three strikes in a row

Rock Climbing Slanguage

Pumping plastic climbing on an indoor practice wall

Whipper long fall

El Choppo getting killed in a fall

Gumby stupid climber

An Elvis uncontrollable shaking and jerking in a muscle as a result of muscle fatigue

Brain bucket helmet

Chickenhead rock outcropping that has a good hold for your hand or foot

Discos rock climbers who wear Lycra

Party ledge large ledge where many climbers can stop and rest during a long or difficult climb

Buildering to climb a building

OCCupaTionAL
SLANGuage

Ax the leading or dominating market maker in a particular stock. This market maker can have a potent impact on the way a stock behaves. There's a thin line between the proper execution of an Ax's responsibility and out-and-out manipulation of a stock.

Dot bomb a play on the expression "dot com," which is a reference to an Internet stock. Dot Bomb is a reference to an Internet stock, too—only this one cost the trader using the term a lot of money.

Fill or Kill also known as a "Fok it!" trade. Stands for "fill-or-kill" order—an order that must be executed immediately at the exact price and quantity specified by the trader—or the specialist or market maker must cancel the order.

Flat indicates a trader has no open positions at the time. Not related to "flat broke," but sometimes indicates a similar result.

Scalper a kind of trader who makes 100 or 200 trades a day, each time just trying to clear $1/16$ or $1/8$. On a lot of 1,000 shares, $1/16$ generates $62.50 in profit, not including commissions. Many people get into day trading because they think they can easily pick off $1/16$ all day long. They usually can't.

Small fortune what most day traders make in their first year of trading—if they start out with a large one.

Take home a trade or "position" that a trader does not liquidate before the end of the trading day. Day trading, by definition, never includes keeping positions open overnight, under the theory that a trader is exposed to too many uncertainties that could cause a sharp drop or rise in a stock's price by the time it opens for trading the next morning.

Teenie Stocks are commonly traded in fractions: ⅞, ½, ¹⁄₁₆, etc. To say "one sixteenth" is a mouthful. Traders abbreviate it by calling it a "teenie," as in, "I just paid 44 and a teenie for that piece of sh*t!"

The Naz shorthand for the exchange managed by the National Association of Securities Dealers, known as the NASDAQ.

Whacked term traders use to describe a trade gone bad. Perhaps borrowed from gangster slang. Both have the same unhappy result: You're dead.

Whipsawed A trader is whipsawed when he or she can do nothing right. When traders go long on a stock and it goes down, then they go short on the same stock and it goes up, they are being whipsawed. Best thing to do is to turn off the computer, go home and come back tomorrow.

Day Trading Slanguage provided by Frank Freudberg, author of the underworld novel *Gasp*.

— © 1999 by Frank Freudberg

Truck Driver Slanguage

Pickle park rest area

Lot lizard truck stop prostitute

Load of dispatcher brains empty trailer

Electric indian yellow flashing construction arrow

Call the travel agent call the dispatcher

The Derby Kentucky

Rotten Apple New York City

The Garbage State New Jersey

The Windy Chicago

Motor City Detroit

The Dirty Side Cleveland

The Big D Dallas

The Big A Atlanta

The Gay Bay San Fransisco

Shakey Los Angeles

Military Slanguage

Peterstain (Viederstain) GI German for good-bye

Donkey smell (Dunkersin) GI German for thank you

Vos is loss at the Bundespost (what is the problem at the post office) GI German for What's up?

We hates (Vi gates) GI German for hello

Nix, nein, nyet, nada, no GI for heck, no

Headshed headquarters office

Exceptional Service Member an idiot who was sneaked into the military by dishonest recruiters

Splittail female soldier

Mud Puppies military police

Sid Criminal Investigation Detachment (vice/homicide military police)

Conus continental United States

Oconus outside the continental United States

Deros going home to the continental United States

Fartsack sleeping bag

Stairwell sleepovers neighbors who get overly friendly with each other

NTC national training center at Ft. Irwin, California

JRTC Joint Readiness Training Center in Arkansas

Horsepills 800 mg Motrin

GP pills general purpose (see Horsepills)

Legal Slanguage

Summerlings or Baby Esq's summer employees. The law school students who "summer" at big firms for about $1,500 a week. For this amount (plus room, board and transportation) they learn the importance of the following terms.

Billable what we can charge a client for time, expense, trip, etc.

Beauty Contest meeting with a client

RFP or RFQ Request for Proposal/Request for Statement of Qualifications. What it really means: Mail a brochure.

Outdoor Business Development party, golf outing, tickets to sporting events

Litigious likes to sue

Southern Medical Slanguage

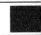

Swinging in the head dizziness

Mixing up stomach pain or not sleeping well

Weasel on the chest wheezing

Womickin' vomiting

Screwing up fetal position when in pain

Flame phlegm

Running off diarrhea

Straddle groin area

Bound up constipated

Depository suppository

Cradle crap that flaky stuff newborns get on their scalps

Years Southern "ears"

Fum-bummelling moving around alot; writhing in pain

Infection nobes swollen glands

Dime attack brand of antihistamine/decongestant

Innovations those fancy newfangled shots to prevent disease

Growth spout Junior just got a lot taller
Pegs/peggin' teeth/teething

Emergency Room Slanguage

GOMER Get Outta My Emergency Room!
Bull in the ring a blockage in the intestines
Smilin' mighty Jesus spinal meningitis
Bore doe (Bordeaux) urine w/blood in it
Captain Kangaroo head of the pediatrics
department
Short-order chefs workers in the
morgue
Goober tumor
Bury the hatchet when a surgeon
accidently leaves something inside a patient
Crispy critter severely burned patient

Silicon Valley Slanguage

Angry fruit salad computer interface designed with way too
many colors
Lasagna software software composed of too many dialog
boxes overlapping each other
Boat anchor an old, old, useless computer

FRED acronym (F***ing Ridiculous Electronic Device) for any electronic device you may like or dislike

Programmer's butt what a programmer gets when they sit too long coding and eating pizza

Spaghetti code poorly written programming code whose "logic" follows a random, illogical path

Uninstalled fired

"The 'G' word" associated with the "go to" command. Frowned upon and almost forbidden.

The Evil Empire of the North Silicon Valley reference to a large computer company located in the Northwestern United States

SLANGuage CROSSwoRd PUZzleS

SLANGUAGE CROSSWORD PUZZLE #1

Puzzle One

Across

1. New Orleans to the locals is _____.
4. A milkshake in Rhode Island is a _____.
5. Beef _____ is a treat in Dallas.
6. South Beach in Miami is _____ to the locals.
9. _____ is a popular seasoning for crabs in Baltimore.
10. Donna Shore is found in the state of _____.
12. _____ is short for Sacramento.
14. _____ is a local beer from Baltimore.
18. The cheer _____ is often heard in Tennessee.
19. Big _____ is a bridge in Michigan.
20. Beef _____ is a popular sandwich in Buffalo.
21. The _____ is a nickname for New Orleans.

Down

2. _____ is 7Up in Milwaukee.
3. In Ohio, many people are _____.
4. Philadelphia's most famous sandwich is a _____.
7. The _____ is a nickname for the Dallas Cowboys.
8. The _____ is short for Tampa Bay's football team.
11. Jacksonville's football team is the _____.
13. _____ is home to the popular Varsity restaurant.
15. A _____ in Milwaukee is a water fountain elsewhere.
16. Downtown Denver is called _____ by the locals.
17. _____ is short for Forest Park in St. Louis, Missouri.

SLANGUAGE CROSSWORD PUZZLE #2

Puzzle Two

Across

1. The _____ is a stadium in Detroit.
3. _____ is a chili dish in Cincinnati.
4. _____ boy is a sandwich in New Orleans.
5. The _____ Ryan is local speak for the Dan Ryan Expressway in Chicago.
7. The _____ is a ballpark in Phoenix.
9. Locals often call Philadelphia _____ for short.
10. _____ is a nickname for Atlanta.
12. The _____ is where the Redskins play.
15. Seattle is nicknamed the _____.
16. _____ Drive is located in Chicago (hint: rhymes w/Slacker).
17. _____ is short for South of the Kingdome in Seattle.
18. Shooting the _____ River is popular in Atlanta.
20. Kansas City is sometimes called _____.
21. _____ is a greeting heard in Honolulu.
23. _____ is a nickname for the "snotty" part of Scottsdale.

Down

1. _____ is another name for garage in New Orleans.
2. _____ Duck was a popular song from the seventies.
6. The center of the universe is _____.
8. A sub sandwich to most is a _____ in Philadelphia.

11. Harvard is occasionally mispronounced _____ by the locals.

13. _____ and God are often synonymous in Chicago.

14. _____ is a reference to burgers from a local chain in the Midwest.

17. Hello in Honolulu to the locals is _____.

18. Folks in Baltimore greet each other with _____.

19. In New York City, _____ is short for south of Houston street.

22. Locals in Tijuana call their town _____ for short.

Answer to Puzzle One

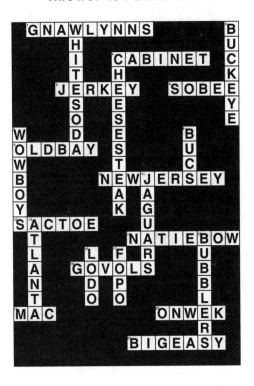

Answer to Puzzle Two